HARRY KNIGHTS

UPPER THAME VALLEY TODAY

**From Cirencester and the Source of the Thames in the west
to Wallingford in the east
From Witney in the north to Swindon and Wantage in the south**

59 new full-colour photographs by
ELISABETH, HARRY and **MARY KNIGHTS**

Ever upon this stage,
Is acted God's calm annual drama,
Gorgeous procession, songs of birds,
Sunrise that fullest feeds and freshens most the soul . . .
The woods, the stalwart trees, the slender tapering trees,
The liliput countless armies of the grass,
The heat, the showers, the measureless pasturages,
The scenery of the snows, the winds' free orchestra,
The stretching light-hung roof of clouds, the clear cerulean and
*   the silvery fringes,*
The high dilating stars, the placid beckoning stars,
The moving flocks and herds, the plains and emerald meadows,
The shows of all the varied lands and all the growths and
products.
WALT WHITMAN

HARRY KNIGHTS PUBLISHER|1985
ABINGDON ON THAMES ENGLAND

GW00360215

INTRODUCTION

The region of the Upper Thames Valley, covered by this book, is from the source of the Thames near Cirencester in the west, Witney in the north, Wallingford in the east and Swindon and Wantage in the south. It is a region in which the river has for many centuries played an important part, as a highway, as a boundary and as a provider of power and of food.

When the Thames was a tributary of the Rhine and Britain was still joined to Europe it was easy for tribes to move into the country from the east. When the Channel separated France from England the Thames made it possible for successive invaders from the Nordic countries to penetrate inland in their boats.

From prehistory the area has been occupied by people attracted by the fertility of the land so that traces are found of Neolithic men, Celts, Gauls, Romans, Saxons, Danes and Normans.

Chalk downs, limestone slopes, and gravel terraces above the Thames, away from the dangers of the wooded valleys provided land which could be settled, easily cultivated and through which travel was much easier than in the marshes and woods below. Flints in the chalk were used to tip arrows and make many different tools. The use of flint to make fire made it possible to clear the land by burning the trees and bushes. Pigs, cows, sheep and oxen, by cropping and manuring the grass, also helped to change the downland.

From about 3,000 BC to 500 BC the country of the Upper Thames seems to have developed peacefully and for this immense period there was an increase in the standard of living of the people. They were able to find the manpower and resources to build burial mounds, such as Wayland's Smithy, and cut impressive figures on the downs such as the White Horse. Societies which can achieve such creations are not exhausting themselves in war. There is an interesting theory about the nature of their society which suggests that at this time the matriarchical earth-worshipping religion was dominant, with fertility rites and the pacific influence of women in ascendance. This Golden Age was only disrupted when the male warrior kings began to worship the use of the force and the glory of war.

With the use of iron and more efficient agriculture, populations grew and Belgic tribes from Gaul came to the Thames area with new weapons and new gods. The Catuvellauni took the north bank of the Thames, the Atrebates the south, leaving the Dobunni, a non-Belgic tribe, on the west of the river.

For 300 years after the conquest of Britain by Claudius in AD 43 the Upper Thames was under Roman rule but the area did not need garrison towns with large numbers of troops, largely because the Dobunni allied themselves with the Romans. The area benefited from the roads that were built, the efficient administration and the introduction of a money economy. As the civilisation of the Romans was adopted by the local farmers they built large and comfortable villas in the Roman style with mosaic floors, heated by underfloor air systems. Remains of these Romano-British houses are found along the Thames and in the valleys of the Evenlode, Windrush and Ock.

When the Romans withdrew in the 4th century AD Saxons and Danes began first to raid and then to settle, but few records of these early Anglo-Saxon and Danish invasions remain.

Alfred the Great (849-99), born at Wantage, established the kingdom of Wessex on the south of the Thames controlling the river crossings at Duxford and Oxford. Christianity came to Wessex in 635 AD when St Birinus baptised Cynegils, the king of Wessex, at Dorchester on Thames.

After long wars against Viking invaders Alfred succeeded in driving them out of Wessex and forcing them to accept Christianity. When he died in 899 he had established a kingdom of England with its base and heartland in the Upper Thames. His achievements in war were

1—*Frontispiece/Infant Thames—Ewen. There are a number of streams in this area near to the source of the Thames which have an abundance of wild flowers growing in them. In this photo of the infant Thames water crowfoot makes a delightful scene in the spring and early summer when the fast current spreads out the long tendrils of the plants.*

immense and the effect of his influence on scholarship, language and the arts endures to this day.

When the dynasty of Alfred died out and Cnut became King of England, Earl Godwin became Lord of Wessex. Harold Godwinson, claimant to the English throne and killed by William the Conqueror at Hastings, drew much of his power from his earldom of Wessex. At the time of the Norman invasion the region of the Upper Thames was the most prosperous and civilised part of England, exceeding Normandy in these respects.

The Normans took possession of the land and built castles and churches, but many of them married daughters of the Saxon ruling classes and were civilised by the society they had conquered.

During the 13th and 14th centuries when there was little fighting in the area, the population expanded and clearance of land led to a great increase in general prosperity. Parish churches were extended and improved by the new Norman architectural styles. The chancel became the responsibility of the vicar and the nave was cared for by the people of the parish. Tombs and other memorials were placed in the churches, aisles were added and screens between chancel and nave were erected to exclude the common people from the chancel.

At this time the only seats in the nave were stone benches built round the walls, provided for the sick and elderly (hence perhaps the saying 'the weakest to the wall'). The building was used for storing communal weapons and tools such as fire-hooks for pulling thatch from burning roofs and the pauper's coffin used to carry corpses to the cemetery.

The prosperity of the area is shown by the tax quotas of 1334 which show that Oxfordshire was the richest county in England and Berkshire the third richest. The Black Death of 1348–9 reduced the population and with the enclosure of land led to many villages being abandoned. The richness of the land still made it possible to produce, with less labour, wool, beef, and hides as well as the usual cereal crops. Flocks of sheep in the country were so numerous that at the beginning of the 16th century there were nine million sheep and about three million people. The wool trade flourished for 300 years and brought wealth to the towns in the valley. There were also associated trades in leather and skins used in the manufacture of gloves, saddlery and leather clothing. The rich wool merchants and landowners built fine houses and rebuilt and endowed the churches with magnificent ornaments.

In the villages there were many craftsmen who practised their trades until about 1914 and sometimes into the 1930s. Most villages had blacksmiths (later motor mechanics), joiners, wheelwrights and hurdle-makers. It was quite usual to find, even in small villages, tailors, shoe-makers, carpenters and masons, making these communities almost self-supporting. Every village had at least one baker who supplied a range of confectionery in addition to bread.

Between 1570 and 1770, another time of prosperity in the country, the villages were rebuilt and improved. Fireplaces, glass windows and upper floors were put into medieval houses, greatly improving the living conditions in them. The towns were growing in size and their larger populations needed the food that was grown in the valley where the water meadows of the Thames provided the best pasture in the country. Cheese alone was sent in huge quantities down the river and one wharf at Buscot was known for many years as the 'Cheese Wharf'.

The oolitic limestone quarried in the area was used to build houses locally, was sent to rebuild London after the fire of 1666 and to build Blenheim Palace and colleges at Oxford.

The Industrial Revolution had small effect on the area. Little coal or other minerals are found in the Upper Thames and the rivers are not swift enough to drive machinery apart from mills. Life continued to be concerned with agriculture and the small trades associated with it. The power of the rich farmers and landed gentry increased as agricultural methods improved with the introduction of turnips, clover, trefoil,

2 Field of Rape. Oilseed rape was not largely grown until about ten years ago but is now the most rapidly expanding crop in the country, covering more than 650,000 acres. It sometimes grows to over six feet with vivid yellow flowers in April and May. The Common Agricultural Policy encourages farmers to plant it since it is hoped that the EEC will become self-sufficient in vegetable oils used in cooking oil and provide a break crop between wheat or barley.

The spectacular splashes of colour which now appear in the countryside have led to

lucerne, sainfoin, improved fertilisation and new machinery. The gentry built fine new houses and laid out landscaped gardens and parks. Parsons who had now improved their position in society lived in large houses near their churches. The landscape of the area was greatly improved by these handsome new buildings, usually built by master craftsmen in local stone.

The appearance of the countryside was greatly changed by the enclosure of common lands which had been carried on from the 15th century. After the dissolution of the monasteries in the 16th century vast tracts of land became available. Oxford colleges bought many of the monastic farms and others passed into the hands of wealthy landowners. This led to yeomen farmers renting land, taking advantage of higher yields from more efficient farming methods and then being able to build better houses. The Government was convinced by agriculturalists of the advantages to

be gained by enclosure and landowners were enabled to ask for private Acts to be passed to allow this to be done. From 1758 to 1882 when the last private enclosure Act of Parliament was passed the process was accelerated and immense areas of arable and waste land were enclosed. Open field farming which had been practised for generations gave great advantages to poor people. In addition to land rented from the lord of the manor they could supplement their living by keeping poultry, pigs, grazing a few cows and generally living off the common land which they did not personally own. When landlords turned out their tenants and cleared away their cottages it caused great misery and led to the creation of poor labourers, often without work.

The rapid increase in population in the late 18th century and early 19th century led to a greater demand from the cities for food. At this time most of the land capable of raising crops was in

differences of opinion between farmers, conservationists and beekeepers. Farmers defend their right to change the look of the countryside if it is profitable, conservationists and ramblers say that the colour is a chemical yellow and the plants obstruct footpaths. Beekeepers differ on the quality of the honey produced from it. There was a lively correspondence in The Times *from May to July 1983 in which all sides of the question were debated.*

5

use and the increase in production had to come from existing farmland. New methods of farming could not be carried out in the open field system and the need for these accelerated the enclosures, leading to the small geometrically-shaped fields we know today with hedges bordering the fields. It is ironic that more mechanical methods of farming requiring large fields and few hedges are now turning many fields back into the open prairie-like expanses of the open field system.

Other changes in the countryside caused by the enclosures were the new roads built to replace the old trackways. Existing paths were usually improved but in some cases new wide roads, forty to sixty feet from hedge to hedge, were provided. The width was necessary because the surfaces were not hard and different parts were used in bad weather. Modern narrower tarmac roads using the post-enclosure routes still have the

wide grass verges indicating their origin. Five Mile Drive in Wolvercote was formerly Horslow Field Way, linking the Woodstock and Banbury main roads and this suburban road retains the broad verges of the original track.

The First Great War with catastrophic losses in the local county regiments had a disastrous effect on the established life in the villages, affecting mostly men between the ages of 18 and 40. The war memorials in the churches show the heart-breaking losses that some families suffered. The loss of manpower in the area accentuated the changes which were already taking place by the use of machines to replace men and the movement of people to nearby towns which needed labour.

Today new industries have been established in and around the Upper Thames bringing new life into the many villages which now house people working in Swindon, the Atomic Energy Research

Establishment, with its various offshoots, and British Leyland in Oxford. There are also small communities of craftsmen in Cirencester and in converted farm buildings such as the Cotswold Woollen Weavers at Filkins and Ardington Workshops.

Gravel and sand extraction from the land between Somerford Keynes and Lechlade has turned large tracts of land into lakes. When the entire area now designated for exploitation has been excavated a series of lagoons will extend for about twelve miles in the manner of the Norfolk Broads.

Nevertheless the beauty and peace of the Upper Thames Valley remain remarkably untouched by the modern world. Along the Thames from Oxford to Lechlade there is no town or village on the river and on either side the lush meadows remain. In many of the villages time appears to have stood still since the 17th century. Among the beautifully mellowed limestone houses a more appropriate sound to hear would be not the roar of jet aircraft but the clatter of coach and horses.

Many of the farm workers who once lived in the villages would be amazed to see how their cottages have been improved and modernised inside although outside they still blend beautifully with their surroundings. The coming of electricity to the smallest hamlet has brought a degree of comfort and assistance to people living there that would seem quite magical to those who built the original houses.

The same rich pastures which fed London for centuries still produce wheat, barley, milk, beef, lamb, cheese, with fruit from the orchards between Harwell and Kingston Bagpuize. The downs that were cleared for flocks of sheep are now also used for training racehorses.

Throughout the whole area the waters of the River Thames and its tributaries enrich and enliven the landscape, softening the outlines of the trees and houses with early mists and lightening the sky with their reflections.

4 *Abingdon—Almshouses. Long Alley (1446), one of the charming almshouses in Abingdon, maintained by Christ's Hospital, an ancient trust (spire of St Helen's Church above). Brick Alley (1718) and Twitty's (1707) are also near the church. After the dissolution of the monastery the care of the sick passed to the Guilds. The original Guilds built bridges at Abingdon and Culham, opening up the town to the riches of the wool trade.*

Abingdon (Photos 4, 5, 6, Map B5) 6 m. s of Oxford on A415

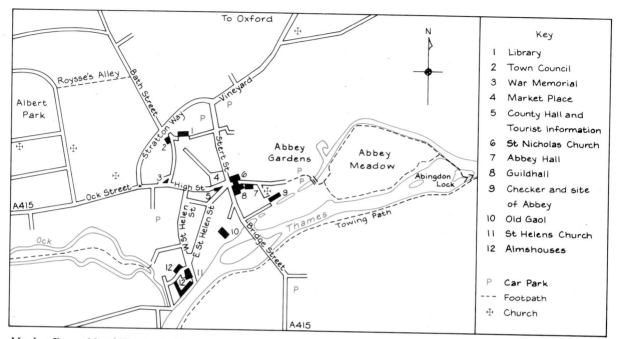

Key

1 Library
2 Town Council
3 War Memorial
4 Market Place
5 County Hall and Tourist Information
6 St Nicholas Church
7 Abbey Hall
8 Guildhall
9 Checker and site of Abbey
10 Old Gaol
11 St Helens Church
12 Almshouses

P Car Park
--- Footpath
♯ Church

Market Day—Mon | *Tourist Infm.*—Market Place | *Parking*—see map | *Toilets*—Shopping Precinct, Abbey Meadows | *P.O.*—High St | *Banks* | *Shopping*—Precinct adjoining Market Place and central streets, good variety of individual shops | *Bookshops*—Knights, High St; Dene, East St Helen St; Architect's Bookshop, Bath St | *Pubs*—about thirty, many with food and real ale | *Hotels* | *Restaurants and cafés* | *Museum*—County Hall, Market Place, open daily 2–5 p.m. | *Sporting Facilities*—Old Gaol, Bridge St (sport and leisure centre including heated indoor swimming pool); Abbey Meadow (outdoor swimming pool open in summer, paddling pool, tennis courts, pitch-and-putt golf, putting); Boating (rowing boats, motor cruisers from Abingdon Boat Centre on bridge and Red Line Cruisers, Wilsham Road); Boat Trips hourly in summer from Abbey Meadows | *Morris Dancing*—Abingdon Traditional Dancers and Mr. Hemmings' Morris Dancers perform in town on various occasions | *Bun-throwing*—Custom perhaps unique to Abingdon: hundreds of buns, baked locally, are thrown by the Mayor and Councillors dressed in robes of office, from top of the County Hall into the Market Place to be caught by the waiting crowd. The number of buns thrown and the enthusiasm and vigour of the councillors seem to be increasing so that the sky at the peak of the performance appears to be raining buns. This ceremony is carried out on any suitable occasion for national rejoicing. The bun-throwing began at the time of the coronation of George III in 1760. Old buns dating back to Victorian times are exhibited in the Town Museum, having been varnished for preservation. They are now freeze-dried at Portsmouth by the same technique which preserves artefacts of the 'Mary Rose'.

Abingdon is one of the fifty towns listed by the Department of the Environment as worthy of special conservation for its architectural merit and many historical associations.

On the approach walls of a subway near the Charter, immense murals depicting famous figures and artefacts from Abingdon's history have been painted by local artist Margaret Jones.

5 *Abingdon—County Hall. Built 1678–83 by Christopher Kempster, master builder to Wren and in his manner if not designed by him. It was built to further the ambition of the town to remain the county town of Berkshire. This ambition was not achieved as Reading became the capital town of the county in 1860. It is undoubtedly one of the finest civic buildings in England of the Stuart period and gives style and elegance to the centre of the town.*

This riverside town of great charm has many fine buildings including a Town Hall of majestic proportions, two beautiful churches and a wealth of interesting pubs. It has probably the best moorings to be found on the Thames (although a charge is now made). There are numerous flower beds in every possible corner as well as flowers in large pots in the main streets. These colourful beds are well-cared-for and do great credit to the local Parks workmen.

The town has had a long and turbulent history, knowing both prosperity and poverty, power and weakness, success and failure. For centuries before the Abbey was founded it was a causewayed camp occupied by farmers, probably a regional tribal centre for the area and in C1 AD the trade of the area came to the river crossing at Abingdon. In Roman times there was a settlement and a market in the town.

The monastery, founded in 695 AD, was twice sacked by the Vikings and then restored by Abbot Ethelwold in 954. In the Doomsday Book the possessions of the Abbey filled four and a half columns. It was the largest ecclesiastical land-owner in Berkshire. Although the Abbey was rich and powerful at that time, only ten traders are recorded outside the Abbey gate.

By 1372 the town had increased in size and the Abbey was now seen by the townspeople as an oppressor, keeping the valuable market rights to itself. The Abbey was attacked by men from Abingdon and Oxford; Northcourt Manor and the Abbey itself were sacked and set on fire. Later twelve ringleaders were hanged at Wallingford and the Abbot was restored to power. The losses suffered by the Abbey were, however, great and from this time its power and influence declined.

After the Dissolution in 1538 the Abbey Church and most of the other buildings were totally destroyed.

St Nicholas Church stands in the Market Place (Photo 6).

St Helen Church The C13 steeple of St Helen is a familiar sight to river travellers as the church stands at the end of East and West St Helen streets at the side of the river. In C15/16 the church was expanded mostly by the Guilds of the town. A great deal of restoration was carried out in 1873 when the heavy pews which now encumber the church were added. Panels on the roof of the inner N aisle show Kings and Prophets and Christ crucified, painted about 1390 and unique in England. The church is unusual in being broader than it is long—108ft wide and 97 ft long. Adjoining church are three almshouses (Photo 4).

County Hall, Market Place, 1678–83 (Photo 5) ground floor now used on Mon. for market stalls, first floor as Museum, open daily 2-5 p.m.

Abbey Hall A new building opened in 1966 with a large hall in which various events are held. It is linked with the older part of the Guildhall which includes the Council Chamber, with a fine collection of paintings. The Roysse Room was originally used by the grammar school students in 1563 when it housed sixty free pupils in its sixty-three-feet length. This handsome room now contains the corporation plate and paintings including one of John Roysse, founder of the school.

Albert Park can be reached by walking through the subway under Stratton Way although the main entrance is off Ock St. It is still an unspoilt Victorian example of a sedate, symmetrical park, given to the town in 1865 by Christ's Hospital. There is a monument of Prince Albert in the centre on a column forty-eight ft high. Large houses similar in style to those in North Oxford surround the park and in adjoining streets there are many other smaller houses of the Victorian period.

Walks A pleasant walk along the River Ock from St Helen Church leads to the Ock Bridge at the junction of Ock St and Drayton Road. The walk starts from a bridge over the Ock at the end of St Helen's Court (off West St Helen St).

From Abingdon Bridge the towpath leads to the lock. Crossing the lock gates the path then leads over two spectacular weirs into the Abbey Meadows. Following the gravel path leads back to the centre of the town via a car park and Abbey Close.

Ampney Crucis, Ampney St Mary, Ampney St Peter (Map B1, B2) on A417 3 to 4 m. E of Cirencester
P.O.|Shop|Pubs with food

Three villages called Ampney by Ampney Brook derive their name from the Saxon 'omenie', meaning brook. The word is pronounced 'Amney' because of this derivation. The villages are fine examples of the use made in the area of the limestone which was quarried locally. The cottage walls, roofs and dry-stone walls were all built of this beautiful stone and many remain today.

The Church of Holy Cross in **Ampney Crucis** includes work from the Saxon period to the C19. The Cross-Head with four carvings now in the churchyard was found in about 1860 bricked up in church wall to protect it from Cromwell's soldiers. Wall panels on the S transept record the hour as well as the date of death of the Pleydell family who lived at Ampney Park from 1561 to 1724. Ampney Park W of the church has a Cotswold manor house of the Jacobean period, with terraced gardens running down to a lake. The gardens are occasionally open to the public.

The village of **Ampney St Mary** is about a mile from the church which now stands isolated in a field by the A417. It seems likely that after the Black Death the villagers who survived moved to a healthier position. Parking is difficult near the church but there is a small lay-by on the opposite side of the road.

The church was built in the C12 and has a bellcote which is 600 years old. The N door, now blocked, has a Norman

7 Ashton Keynes. The Thames, with the source about six miles away, is still only a stream which flows through the village. Several houses in the main street have small bridges across the river and near the old mill (now a private house) there is a (frequently-photographed) group of attractive buildings. On the right a path leads by a line of fine chestnut trees to Holy Cross Church.

lintel with a unique carved design showing the Lion of Righteousness triumphing over the agents of the devil. There are traces everywhere of the rich wall paintings which formerly adorned the church. When it was disused from 1879 to 1913 a forest of ivy covered the building and it was then given the name 'The Ivy Church'.

A small female figure (about twelve inches high) above the C15 font of the Church of **Ampney St Peter** is perhaps a Saxon fertility goddess. Other Saxon work is the s wall and the round-headed arch of the tower. The gabled roof of the low w tower and small rectangular windows are Norman. Sir Gilbert Scott restored and extended the church in 1878. There is a C14 cross in the churchyard.

Ardington (Map C5) off A417 2 m. E of Wantage
P.O.|Shop|Butcher|Pub. with food
At the foot of the Downs among fine trees, contains many cottages built in the 1880s by the local Lockinge estate then owned by Lord Wantage.

Ardington Workshops include a potter, a leather worker, a rush and cane worker, cabinet makers in pine and hardwood, an engineer (dealing with diverse jobs—from making keys for old church locks to sheet metal work), a picture framer. There is also 'Intermediate Technology Transport' which provides low-cost transport for countries in the Third World. An interesting and encouraging use of old farm buildings now housing various crafts and bringing life back to the village. When the project

is completed there will be a large variety of craftsmen in the workshops.

Robert Loyd-Lindsay won the VC in the Crimean War, rebuilt Ardington and Lockinge (a nearby village) and was a most successful farmer and land-owner. He was also an MP and head of a number of local organisations. In 1885 he was made Lord Wantage of Lockinge. He died childless in 1901 and death duties broke up the estate. His memorial cross is on the Ridgeway above Wantage.

Ardington House is an C18 grey and red-brick building of three stories and seven bays with a projecting three-bay centre. There is a decorated pediment and a stone doorway with a complex top. The side of the house by the garden is similar except for the doorway and the addition of a wooden veranda. The house is open to visitors by appoint-ment—May to September.

Holy Trinity Church has a prominent Victorian spire on the N tower and a beautiful N door of about 1200 with many mouldings and dogtooth carvings. The church was expensively restored in 1887 and has many furnishings of that period.

Ashbury (Map C3) at junction of B4507 and B4000 6 m. E of Swindon
P.O.|Shop|Hotel
The Icknield Way passes through Ashbury, and the Ridgeway is about a mile to the S. Set among trees on a steep slope of the Downs overlooking the Vale of the White Horse it is in a beautiful situation. *St Mary's Church*, reached through an avenue of trees, is built of chalk and brown stone and is Norman in origin. The Manor House, a rare survival of the C15, is also built of chalk and stone. There are several thatched cottages and other charming houses in the village, making it an ideal place from which to explore the Ridge-way and local archaeological sites.

There is a pleasant short walk to Upper Mill with its attractive duck pond and stream by a path starting at the Free Church.

Wayland's Smithy is E of the village (see **The Ridgeway**).

Ashton Keynes (Photo 7, Map 1) 6 m. S of Cirencester
P.O.|Shop|Pubs|Garage
Holy Cross Church. William Butterfield restored the building in 1877 but parts are still of the original Norman and Perpendicular periods. Remains of a double moat which once encircled the church and Church Farm can be seen adjoining the church.

There are four crosses in the village standing at the end of Church Walk, by the *White Hart Inn*, by Smith's shop and in the churchyard. It is not known why they were erected although they may have been 'preaching crosses' or 'stages' at which funeral processions rested.

Bablockhythe (Map A5) off B4449 2½ m. SE of Stanton Harcourt on the Thames: accessible only by car from B4449, also on foot from Cumnor by ferry across river.
Pub. with food|Camp site|Caravans
A pub. stands by the side of the Thames at a place which has been a crossing of the river for many centuries. At one time a ferry boat carried cars across the river but a boat is now being worked (powered by an outboard motor) for passengers only.

A large and intrusive mobile home site adjoins the pub. and lines the river bank for some way. However there is still enough of the river magic about the place to recall the spirit of Matthew Arnold who wrote of the scholar gypsy 'crossing the stripling Thames at Bab-lock-hithe/Trailing in the cool stream thy fingers wet . . .'

Bampton (Map B4) at junction of A4095 and B4449 6 m. SW of Witney
P.O.|Banks|Garage|Good range of shops|Parking—centre of town|*Toilets*—Town Hall|*Pubs* with food and accommodation|*Restaurants|Cafés*
Bampton Arts Centre (closed Mon. and Wed.)—Town Hall
Bampton, a quiet handsome stone-built village, was once an important market town and the magnificent church reflects the wealth of the area. The population

declined during the C18 as other markets in nearby towns increased in size and although there were cottage industries making gloves and jackets no major industry developed there. The most famous activity in the village now is the Morris Dancing which has been carried on for at least 350 years. When they perform on the Spring Bank Holiday they march to the church bearing a cake. At one time pieces of cake were sold as aids to fertility.

St Mary's Church, one of the largest and finest in the area, stands in a close surrounded by three former vicarages and the old deanery—the oldest house in the village. The spire is supported in a striking way by statues on pedestals of clustered shafts at each corner linked to the spire by small flying buttresses. The church was restored by Ewan Christian in 1867–9 when the interior was scraped.

In the centre of the village the Town Hall, built in 1838, now houses the *Bampton Arts Centre*. There are several very well built and attractive houses in the village.

Binsey (Photos 8, 9, Map A5) off A420, approached by Binsey Lane ½ m. W of Oxford railway station

Perch Inn Only pub in the hamlet, was recently badly damaged by fire but rebuilt as before with thatched roof, can be approached from the river, pleasant gardens with dove-cote, good food available. When boating on the river one of the most attractive places to moor for the night is at the *Perch* where the lights of Oxford can be seen across the wide expanse of *Port Meadow* —a memorable sight.

St Margaret's Church Approached by a road bordering the few houses in the hamlet, to the left of the pub about ½ mile in length, ending in an avenue of chestnut trees. A small rustic church with chancel, nave and C13 central belfry, S doorway late C12. The church is heavily shaded by the surrounding trees and the rather gloomy, mysterious setting prepares the visitor for the miraculous legend of St Frideswide with which the church is associated.

Black Bourton (Map A3) off B4020 3 m. N of Radcot
Pub
St Mary's Church (C14), alterations made in C15, restored in 1866. Late C12 round font and stone pulpit of C15. Distinguished by unusual number of wall paintings of late C13. They include Coronation of the Virgin and Annunciation, St Christopher, Tree of Jesse, and Adoration of the Three Wise Men. Near the entrance to the church-yard there is a group of graves, with uniform headstones, of a number of RAF men most of whom died in the Second World War. There is an RAF base nearby at Brize Norton.

A house by the church has built into the wall a crest and a relief of armour and helmet from Bourton Place, the manor house of the Hungerfords, de-molished in about 1800, also a date stone of 1655 and the initials I.T.M. It was formerly the *Horse and Groom Inn*.

Buckland (Map B4) off A420 10 m. W of Abingdon
P.O.|Shop|Pub.
A compact, well-kept village built of limestone with many fine trees. The cottages are in scale and in harmony with the larger houses so that the whole place has a tranquil and satisfactory appearance. The setting of the village, overlooking the Thames valley and the surrounding farms, adds to the general picturesque scene.

The Throckmorton family who took over the manor in about 1690 had a new house built in 1757 by Wood the younger who also built houses in Bath. Buckland House is not open to the public, being used as a college.

St Mary is an exceptionally wide church of the C12/C13 with Victorian additions. The S transept is lavishly and expensively decorated in a startling fashion with every conceivable Victorian embellishment. It was paid for in memory of his late wife by William West, a director of the GWR.

A mile N of the village, on the road to Bampton, Tadpole Bridge with a single arch over the Thames is set in

8 *Binsey—St Margaret's Church, The Healing Well.* This is the well at the side of the church which legend claims was called forth by St Frideswide after Prince Algar had been blinded because of his pursuit of her. When she struck the ground with her staff the water which poured out restored his sight. In the Middle Ages the well was thought to be capable of curing many diseases, particularly those of the eyes and infertility. The last royal visitors were Henry VIII and Katharine of Aragon. In the C17 the water was sold for a guinea a bottle, and today there are still tributes to its healing powers in the visitors' book in the church.

The Treacle Well or Treacle Mine of Binsey is well-known in Oxford and is mentioned by the Dormouse in 'Alice in Wonderland'. The Middle English word 'triacle' means 'antidote'. The 'Treacle Bible' or Bishop's Bible of 1568 translated 'balm' as 'treacle' in *Jeremiah*.

9 *Binsey—St Margaret's Church, Carving of St Margaret. This wooden carving, attributed to Eric Gill, is on the inside of the pulpit because it was deemed liable to inflame the passions of the congregation. To the prudish it might be thought to be sensual since the saint's draped breasts are clearly shown. She is said to have been swallowed by a dragon but disgorged when she made the sign of the cross. As the figure holds a cross and rises from a dragon-like creature it must be St Margaret and not St Frideswide as stated in some guide-books. Our efforts to authenticate the carving as the work of Eric Gill have not been successful. It is not listed in books about him and the folds of the cloak are not as deep as in his other work. On the outside of the pulpit there is a more conventional carving of St Margaret. The positions of the carvings have, apparently, been changed depending on the attitudes of the incumbents—'modern' vicars have fixed the 'Eric Gill' outside the pulpit and 'traditional' priests have moved it inside.*

solitude in the river meadows without any apparent reason for its existence or for its name. It may have been built in the late C18 to compensate the owner of a weir which was removed. The *Trout Inn* near the bridge serves food and has a camping and caravan site.

Buscot (Photo 10, Map B3) on A417
2 m. SE of Lechlade
P.O.|Shop|Pub.|Picnic Area|Car Park—NT
Buscot village is situated away from the river near which the church still stands.

At the entrance to the village from the A417 there is a village hall with a clock tower (about 1890) and a covered well with a standpipe and tap in working order. The hall was erected by the 1st Lord Faringdon who also built several cottages which stand in the same street by the side of a stream. There is a car park on the right.

A path by the side of Lock Farm House leads to *St Mary's Church* through a lychgate. The church has a C13 nave and chancel arch, a perpendicular tower and a C13 chancel altered in C18. The pulpit has a Flemish triptych on three

10 *Buscot Weir, Lock Cottage and Pool behind the Lock. This is an ideal place for a picnic as the area round the pool is kept clear of cars, which must be left in a park on the right in the village. Several fine houses seen on the way to the lock are now maintained by the National Trust. Near the lock is the picturesque original weir cottage.*

17

panels, early C16. There is a stained glass E window by Burne-Jones, representing the Good Shepherd, and a splendid wooden Spanish lectern. By the side of lock cottage a path leads to Buscot Lock from where there are many other pleasant walks, including one along the towpath to Kelmscott.

The Old Parsonage, a fine stone house (1703) owned by the NT is open on Wed. afternoons by appointment.

Buscot House was built in about 1780 by Edward Loveden Townsend who developed the estate and was a successful farmer. He produced large quantities of cheese which he shipped down the Thames from a warehouse at Buscot Wharf (known as the 'Cheese Wharf'). In 1859 the house and estate were bought by Robert Campbell, a rich Australian. He introduced modern farming methods

well ahead of his times, building a narrow-gauge railway round the estate. He planted acres of sugarbeet to produce alcohol distilled on an island called Brandy Island, near Buscot Lock. Campbell also built a reservoir to irrigate the estate, a mill for oil cake, a gas works and a telegraph system. Nothing now remains of these industries with the exception of a concrete-walled barn in Buscot village, built in 1870.

In 1889 Buscot was bought by Alexander Hamilton, later 1st Lord Faringdon. He ran the estate by conventional methods and also rebuilt much of the village. The Faringdon family assembled a fine and varied collection of furniture, *objets d'art* and paintings including the Burne-Jones Briar Rose series. The house, open to the public, is beautifully furnished, providing a splendid setting for the magnificent Faringdon collection.

The attractive gardens were laid out by the 1st Lord Faringdon in a formal and Italianate fashion, and were extended in the 1930s. There is a chain of stairways, paths, basins and canals linking the house with the great lake. Fountains and miniature cascades, hump-backed balustraded bridges, marble seats and statuary add variety to the grand design. Work still continues on the gardens including a redesigning of the kitchen gardens.

Castle Eaton (Photo 11, Map B2) off A419 3½ m. NE of Cricklade

P.O.|Shop|Pub with food, riverside garden
Stands by the Thames in good farming country, distinguished by an interesting church overlooking the Thames and an exceptionally ugly iron bridge over the river. The *Red Lion Inn* is a Georgian red-brick building with a stone-slated roof.

Charney Bassett (Photo 12, Map B4) off A420 8 m. W of Abingdon
P.O.|Shop|Pub
Was once a possession of Abingdon Abbey and suffered by having to pay parish rates to Longworth, leaving the villagers with little money to repair

12 River Ock at Charney Bassett, an idyllic spot about halfway between the source E of Great Coxwell and the confluence with the Thames at Abingdon. Touching no other town, it meanders through the meadows of the Vale. The Ock Valley was once a marsh and is crossed by many streams, the villages having been built on patches of firm ground. The "ey" in Charney is the Saxon suffix for island.

their church. Stands on the River Ock which at one time provided salmon and crayfish.

St Peter's Church, next to the C13 Manor House, has a small C16 stone turret and a perpendicular nave roof. The s doorway has a moulding with a tympanum inside showing a standing man holding two gryphons and being bitten by them. The man was said to be Alexander the Great but this is now discounted. The date of the carvings has not been definitely placed and may be as early as the Norse Viking period. A curious bell-cote was added during the reign of James I.

Childrey (Photo 13, Map C4) on B4001 3½ m. w of Wantage
P.O.|Shops|Pubs|Garage
Childrey was one of the homes of the Fettiplace family which died out in 1806. From C13 this family owned many properties in the area, moving to Childrey in 1435. There are many reminders in the village of the family such as the Fettiplace Almshouses (1526), Sir John Fettiplace's School (1732) and memorials in the church.

St Mary's Church overlooking the vale is a large cruciform church with perpendicular tower to the N of the village, approached through an avenue of trees.

13 *Childrey Pond. In the centre of Childrey this large well-kept duck-pond is by the side of the village green near several attractive houses of various periods.*

Cirencester (Photos 14, 15, Map B1) at junction of A417, A419, A429, A433

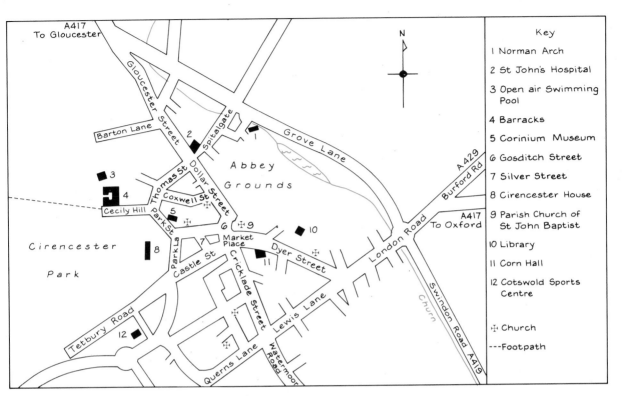

Key
1 Norman Arch
2 St John's Hospital
3 Open air Swimming Pool
4 Barracks
5 Corinium Museum
6 Gosditch Street
7 Silver Street
8 Cirencester House
9 Parish Church of St John Baptist
10 Library
11 Corn Hall
12 Cotswold Sports Centre

⊬ Church
---Footpath

Market Days—Mon. Fri.|*Antique Market*, Corn Hall—Fri.|*Craft Market*, Corn Hall—Sat.|*Tourist Infm.*—Corn Hall|*Parking*—several, well signed| *Toilets*—Forum car park, Abbey Grounds |*P.O.*|*Banks*|*Garages*|*Supermarkets*| *Shopping*—exceptionally good for town of this size|*Bookshops*—Baily & Woods, Market Place; W.H. Smith, Castle St; Town Bookseller, Cricklade St; Paul Weller, Dollar St|*Hotels*|*Restaurants*| *Cafés*|*Pubs with food*

Corinium Museum, Park St, recently redesigned, from prehistory and Roman period to Saxon and Medieval times. One of the finest collections of Roman remains in the country including several large and beautiful mosaics.

Cirencester Workshops, Brewery Court, Cricklade St. Interesting, attractive development in town centre containing Arts Centre, Gallery, Craft Shops, Coffee Shop with food, eleven independent workshops and study room. Workshops are occupied by about twenty-five full-time professional craftsmen who can be seen practising their skills.

Sporting Facilities—Cotswold Sports Centre, Tetbury Rd (swimming pools, indoor sports facilities); Polo (weeks in May, June, August—Cirencester Park); Swimming, open air, reached by footpath from Cecily Hill and Park St.

St John the Baptist Church (Photo 15) built in C12 outside an Abbey which was destroyed in 1539 by Henry VIII.

Royal Agricultural College First agricultural college in the country, on sixty-acre site between Stroud Rd and Tetbury Rd. College farms 1300 acres.

Corinium Dobunnorum was the second largest town in Britain during Roman times—the name deriving from the nearby river Churn and from the British tribe of Dobunni who were living in the area when the Romans arrived. Their tribal symbol was a white horse which was cut into the chalk hillside at Uffington.

Important Roman roads crossed at the town—Foss Way, Akeman St and Ermin Way. Legions were stationed in a fort which was s of the present-day Avenue. In the C4 it was a splendid

14 *Cirencester—View of Cirencester House and Park from the top of the parish church, reached by climbing the 162-ft-high tower. Parts of the staircase are in darkness and without a handrail.*

wealthy city with all the amenities of Roman urban civilisation—wide streets, public buildings, baths, amphitheatre and luxurious private houses.

During Saxon times the town retained its importance and a church was built near the present site of the parish church. In 1142–46 the Augustinian Abbey of St Mary and the parish church of St John were built, the Abbot assuming authority over the affairs of the town.

In the Middle Ages Cirencester grew in importance as a centre for the rich wool, weaving and cloth-making trades. The Abbot, however, prevented the town from becoming a Borough and was accused of burning the Royal Charter which would have given authority to the people. However, as was the practice in other towns, charities were set up to help old and poor people, enabling rich

merchants to become benefactors.

The Guilds of skilled men were also influential in matters affecting the town and its affairs.

At the dissolution of the monasteries in 1539 the Abbey and its church were completely destroyed and nothing now remains except a Norman gatehouse in the Abbey grounds.

During the Civil War in the C17 Cirencester supported Cromwell but was taken by Prince Rupert in 1643. The parliamentary forces later recaptured the town.

The town expanded in C18 when several schools were founded and fine houses built, many of which remain today. A branch of the Thames and Severn Canal reached the town in 1789 but both this and the railway line have now disappeared.

15 *Cirencester—St John the Baptist Church. Magnificent parish church built in the C12 outside an Abbey which was destroyed in 1539 by Henry VIII. It has a nave rebuilt and raised in the early C16 by local cloth-merchants, with a fine seven-light window above chancel arch. C15 stone pulpit is a delicate wineglass shape with pierced panels decorated in red and green. Great tower built from 1400–1430 has no spire although first intended, and two immense spur-buttresses had to be built to support the tower. Contains most interesting set of church plate in the country. Boleyn Cup of 1535 is on permanent display. Church stands in busiest part of town but behind it is a quiet churchyard and the restful expanse of Abbey Grounds looking out over a lake formed by River Churn. The enjoyment of this pastoral scene is heightened by the unusual setting near the bustle of the Market Place.*

Today the town is a busy, thriving centre for the S Cotswolds with a variety of attractive shops. The *Market Place* has a dignified Georgian atmosphere with many handsome buildings although the ground floors are often now occupied by shops.

From the Market Place *Gosditch St* (a short street W of the church) leads into *Dollar St* with C17/18 stone houses, one occupied by Paul Weller, new and antiquarian bookseller. *Coxwell St*, off Dollar St, has a wealth of old houses, unsurpassed in the Cotswolds, culminating in an imposing C18 three-storied ashlar house which has seven mullioned and transomed windows. On the other side of the street are gabled stone cottages, said to have been occupied by poor weavers, while the grander houses opposite were the homes of richer wool merchants.

Thomas St contains the Weavers Hall or St Thomas's Hospital founded by Sir William Nottingham who died in 1437 and the Temperance Hall built in Gothic style in 1846. In *Spitalgate*, off Dollar St, are the remains of St John's Hospital founded by Henry II—four bays of a transitional Norman arcade. *Gloucester St* (continuation of Dollar St) has other interesting houses of the C17/18.

Cecily Hill is the main approach to *Cirencester Park* and this unusually wide street has large comfortable houses of various periods built in mellow limestone. At the end of the street are the Old Barracks (1857) with tower, turret and lancet windows—now no longer in military use but being offered for use as a store.

The Park, open to the public, is the finest and probably the largest example of formal landscaping with geometrical avenues which preceded the naturalistic gardens of Capability Brown. The estate is vast—about 3,000 acres—and the Broad Ride, over 150ft wide for 1¼ miles, runs through the park for nearly five miles. Seven rides meet near a stone summer house designed by Pope and ten rides meet at the Horse Guards (two ornamental arches). The estate was designed by the first Earl Bathurst with the help of Alexander Pope. The Earl not only laid out the magnificent avenues

with their trees, statues and romantic buildings but also introduced modern farming methods. He was more interested in farming than in architecture. *Cirencester House* (not open to the public), built in 1714–18 by local masons and carpenters, is a plain structure incorporating parts of the original Elizabethan Manor house which stood on the site. After the mansion was built Lord Bathurst asked Pope, 'How comes it to look so oddly bad?'. An enormous elliptical yew hedge forty ft high conceals the building from Park St.

Clifton Hampden (Photo 16, Map B6)
4 m. SE of Abingdon on A415
P.O.|Shop|Pubs with food|Garage|Parking and Toilets opposite Barley Mow pub|*Swimming* in the river|*Picnic area* by river
Church of St Michael and All Angels (Photo 16)

Clifton Hampden is an attractive riverside village with ample parking—very popular in the summer. G.H. Gibbs became Lord of the Manor in 1842 and completely restored and modernised the estate. He built a new manor house, new cottages for the tenants and the bridge over the Thames, which replaced a ferry. Until 1946 a toll was levied at the bridge. There are a number of pretty C16/17 cottages in the village. Jerome K. Jerome wrote 'Three Men in a boat' at the *Barley Mow Inn*, of cruck construction, recently badly damaged by fire and rebuilt.

Coleshill (Map B3) on B4019 2½ miles NE of Highworth, SW of Faringdon
P.O.|Shop
A picturesque village on a hill over the River Cole with model houses built by the second Earl of Radnor in about 1870. The village pub called *The Radnor Arms* recalls this connection. *All Saints Church* stands on rising ground behind a small green and has a perpendicular tower, a transitional and Early English nave, chancel and S chapel. The church was restored in the C19. Well preserved stone-built cottages with stone tiles, along the hilly street make a very pleasant picture.

Only four pairs of C17 gate-piers now remain of the magnificent house in the village partly designed by Inigo Jones. The house itself was destroyed by fire in 1952.

Cuckoo Penn Plantation, ½ m. E, is a good National Trust picnic area with fine beech trees. *Badbury Hill* (with car park) also National Trust, lies a mile further along the B4019 towards Faringdon. This is an Iron Age encampment commanding superb panoramic views of the Thames and Ock valleys, seen from a path which runs round the perimeter. The high and flat part of the camp is planted with beech trees and in season has a carpet of bluebells.

Coln St Aldwyns (Photo 17, Map A2) off A417 3 m. N of Fairford
P.O./Shops/Inn with accommodation and food

An unspoilt and little-visited village of considerable charm.

Compton Beauchamp (Photo 18, Map C3) off B4507 8 m. W of Wantage
St Swithun's Church is most attractive, built of chalk blocks dressed with limestone, roofed with limestone slates. Unusual use of soft white chalk gives a fresh, clean look to this modest church with no spire but a pyramid roof to its C13 unbuttressed tower. Has a high narrow nave with white painted roof, modern (1900) chancel painting with vines, E window palm fronds also modern by same artist, Lydia Lawrence. E window also contains C14 crucifixus.

Cotswold Wild Life Park (Map A3) off A361 7 m. N of Lechlade
Contains a collection of exotic mammals,

16 Clifton Hampden— Church of St Michael and All Angels. The C13 church which stood on this site, on a cliff overlooking the river, was restored by Gilbert Scott in 1844 and 1866. Five flights of steps lead up to the church which contains a spectacular memorial in the opulent 'founder's chapel' to G. H. Gibbs who paid for the restoration.

17 *Coln St Aldwyns. A small green by the River Coln at the foot of the main street which is lined by attractive limestone cottages. Up the hill, an inn, converted from a C14 malthouse serves excellent meals. The church, Norman in origin, heavily restored in 1853, contains a memorial in the E window to John Keble, curate from 1825–1835.*

tropical birds, reptiles and insects with landscaped gardens, a narrow-gauge railway, woodland walks and an adventure playground. Also provides picnic areas, a licensed bar and restaurant. There are 120 acres of gardens and parkland round Bradwell Grove, an early C19 manor house. The old dining room is now an animal brass-rubbing centre and the drawing room is used for meetings and lectures. The Park is open from 10 a.m. every day except Christmas Day, and provides a very enjoyable day out for the family.

Cricklade (Photo 19, Map B2) off A419 at junction of B4040 and B4041 7 m. SE of Cirencester
P.O. | Usual Shops also excellent *DIY store | Banks | Garage | Parking*—centre of town in High St | *Toilets*—High St | *Hotels | Cafés | Pubs with food | Museum | Leisure Centre*

St Samson Church Dedicated to a Celtic saint and missionary from Cornwall, partly built in Anglo-Saxon times. The great tower built in the Tudor period has four great pinnacles resting on large piers and can be seen for many miles across the water meadows.

High St A wide, pleasant street in the centre with many interesting houses of C18/19.

St Mary's Church A much-restored church originally Norman, now disused and its future uncertain as alternative uses are being considered. There is an interesting cross in the churchyard, C14 with a sculptured four-sided lantern head.

Ermin Way, a Roman road from Cirencester, passes near the town and the same line is now followed by the bypass. There is evidence of a Romano-British settlement here and King Alfred fortified the town with an earthen rampart, replaced by a stone wall in the

C11. Until the early C19 the river was navigable in the higher reaches. The early spelling of Cricklade was Cricca-gelad (the place with wharves where the river may be crossed).

The town is a quiet agricultural place now that the bypass has taken the traffic away. There is also a National Nature Reserve at North Meadow on the other side of the river which preserves the fritillaries (snakes-heads) which bloom in late spring.

Culham (Map B5) off A415 2 m. SE of Abingdon
P.O.|Shop|Pubs with food|Parking near lock on road to Sutton Bridge
St Paul's Church **W** tower was rebuilt in 1710 but the main part of the church is a Victorian building.

Manor House —partly C15—formerly a grange of the Abbey of Abingdon. Various parts of the house were rebuilt in C17. In the garden there is a rectangular dove-cote built in 1685 of brick and stone with 4000 nesting places.

Culham is now famous as the site of JET (Joint European Torus). This is the largest single project of the coordinated nuclear fusion research programme of the European Atomic Energy Community (Euratom) aimed at proving the feasibility of nuclear fusion as a new energy source. In other words scientists are trying to find out how to produce energy by ramming atoms of hydrogen together to produce helium and in so doing they will create heat eight times as hot as the sun. Inside ten-foot-thick concrete walls a giant 'kettle' will heat hydrogen to 100m. degrees. Little of the buildings of JET

18 *Compton Beauchamp. St Swithun's Church stands alongside the moat of Compton House (C16/18), a handsome stone-faced building, with an oblong courtyard.*

can be seen from the road and it is open to the public only on special occasions. To educate the children of the scientists at JET who come from various countries of Europe, the former Culham College is now The European School.

The Thames is near the village and there is a lock and footpath along the river which leads to Sutton Courtenay by crossing a bridge. It is also possible to walk to Clifton Hampden or Abingdon by following the towpath.

Cumnor (Map A5) off A420 3 m. W of Oxford
P.O.|Shops|Pubs with food
St Michael's Church stands on high ground—C18 tombstones in surrounding graveyard. Contains a splendid circular oak staircase inside the tower built in 1685. The building still retains the shape and has many details of the transitional late C12 despite many later additions.

The early features are in the tower and chancel arch. There is a monument in the chancel in Purbeck marble to Anthony Forster (1572) who is alleged to have murdered Amy Robsart. She lived in Cumnor Place, now demolished, near the church.

The village has limestone cottages, and an old stone inn with gabled wings and moulded window openings called *The Bear and Ragged Staff*. When Abingdon Abbey was surrendered to Henry VIII the last Abbot, Thomas Pentecost, was given the manor of Cumnor with a pension of £200 a year.

Farmoor Reservoir (378 acres) N of the village, supplying water to the Oxford area, is also used for sailing and fishing.

Didcot (Photo 20, Map C5) at junction A4130 and B4016 14 m. S of Oxford
Market Day—Fri. Sat. | *Tourist Infm.*— 128 Broadway | *Parking and Toilets* | *P.O.*

19 *Cricklade—St Samson's Church.*

20 *Didcot Power Station with its two high chimneys and six cooling towers dominates the skyline in the whole area, being visible for many miles around. Seen from a distance through luminous valley mists the harsh outlines of the towers are softened so that they appear as industrial castles. A nearer view shows a grimmer picture but one which gives a vivid appreciation of the impressive bulk of the station.*

21 *Dorchester on Thames—Abbey Church of St Peter and St Paul. Magnificent late-C12 cruciform church over 200 ft long, stands partly on the site of the Abbey, demolished after the dissolution in 1536. The monastic records were destroyed at that time and early history of the building is largely unknown. Major alterations made in C13/14/17, including rebuilding the choir in C14. This was carried out with great originality and the sculptured tracery cannot be matched anywhere in Europe. The church was restored from 1845 to 1874 by James Cranston, William Butterfield and G.G. Scott. The impressive lychgate with immense arched timbers was designed by W.M. Butterfield.*

Banks|*Garages*|*Usual Shops*, mostly in Broadway|*Hotel*|*Pubs*|*Cafés*|*Cinema*—Broadway|*Swimming Pool*—Edmonds Park|*Railway Station*—very good service, frequent trains to most parts of the country.

Didcot Railway Centre Entrance through Didcot Railway Station: railway history shown in all its features; covers sixteen acres; engine shed, workshop, coaling stage, turntable, carriage restoration and storage shed; two demonstration lines used on operating days; complete small station, with signal box and level crossing; a unique creation of the seven-ft broad gauge railway is under construction; twenty-three steam locomotives, many already restored to working order; refreshments; book and souvenir shop; picnic areas; all Didcot Steam Days offer a continuous programme of operations, with free rides in steam trains; admission prices vary with events. Open Easter-October Mon.-Fri. 12-4.30, Sat. 12-5, Sun. 11-5

Didcot is a village overwhelmed by the railway, later by the Power Station (Photo 20) and further expansion is planned.

Dorchester on Thames (Photo 21, Map B6) now bypassed by A423 9 m. SE of Oxford
P.O.|*Shops*, many antique shops|*Garage*|*Parking*|*Toilets*—Bridgend *Hotels*|*Pubs with food*|*Teashop* in Old School House adjoining Abbey Church (open in summer)|*Museum* in Old School House (open Easter–September at various times)
Abbey Church of St Peter and St Paul (Photo 21) Inside the church the three large windows contain beautiful medieval coloured glass including the famous Jesse window in the N of the chancel. The lead font (about 1170) is one of the best-preserved in England and is the only one belonging to a monastic church to survive the Reformation. A stone cross (C14/15) restored in about 1872 stands in the churchyard. In the Lady Chapel is a shrine designed in 1964 by F. Russell Cox which is in the original form and contains fragments of the C14 shrine destroyed at the Reformation.

One of the finest and best-preserved

effigies in the country is that of Sir John Holcombe, a C13 crusader who died in the second crusade. He is shown cross-legged and drawing his sword.

The Cloister Garden on the N side of the church provides a peaceful and attractive area from which the oldest parts of the church can be seen.

Toll House and Bridge The octagonal Toll House and bridge were built in 1813/1815. The bridge, which crosses the Thame (a tributary of the Thames) replaces a medieval one at Bridge End.

Until the town was bypassed in 1982 all the Oxford-to-Henley traffic passed through the picturesque main street and this made it impossible to appreciate the buildings in this charming place. Now that peace has been restored the timbered houses, thatched cottages and ancient inns can be properly seen. Opposite the churchyard is the *George Inn* (about 1500 with gabled front, an overhanging first floor and an arch leading to a courtyard now used for parking. The building is timber-framed, stuccoed and with sash windows. The *White Hart Hotel*, with narrow timbered gables, also in the High St, has the date 1691 on the building but may be much older. There is also a wealth of attractive houses built in the C15/16/17 in the main street and in the lanes and paths leading off the High St there are many other charming buildings well worth seeing.

A pleasant and interesting walk leads from Bridge End through lanes and fields passing Dyke Hills to Day's Lock on the Thames and to *Little Wittenham* (see **Little Wittenham**).

Overy Mill and Manor House, built in the C17/18 can be reached by walking down Queen St (off High St), along Manor Farm Road and across the fields crossing the River Thame. This leads to the bridge over the river and to the High St.

The strategic position of the town near the junction of the rivers Thame and Thames has attracted settlements since neolithic times and there are exceptionally rich archaeological remains in the area. To the S across the river is Castle Hill, an Iron Age hill fort on top of the Sinodun Hills which was abandoned in the late Iron Age. Dyke Hills, also S of the village.

22 Duxford. The ford here existed for centuries before the Romans and although the Thames now flows to Shifford Lock through a cut the crossing still exists on a backwater, reached by a narrow footpath from Duxford. Large paving stones are set in the river which in summer is only inches deep. From the ford the water drops about three ft to continue on its way. Large willows hang over the left bank of the river crossing.

was then used as a fortress in pre-Roman times. This defended settlement has not been explored and if excavated would without doubt yield many archaeological treasures.

The Roman town was established as an administrative centre soon after the conquest on the road between Silchester and Alchester. The alignment of the Roman occupation is still shown in the layout of the village.

Bishop Birinus was sent to England in 635 to convert the people and was given Dorchester by King Cynegils. Birinus founded the cathedral and in 1170 it became an Augustinian Abbey and the existing church was built. In 1536 the monastic buildings were demolished but the Abbey Church remained to be pur-

chased by Richard Beauforest who presented it to the parish.

Down Ampney (Map B2) off A419 6 m. SE of Cirencester
P.O.|Shop
Ralph Vaughan Williams was born in the Old Vicarage in 1872. He commemorated the place of his birth by the tune 'Down Ampney' to the words 'Come Down O Love Divine'.

All Saints Church (C13) is at the S end of the village. Contains two excellent monuments to Sir Nicholas de Valers in coat of mail with long sword and shield, head on pillow, feet on dog, legs crossed: Margaret de Valers is at his side. There is an abundance of heavy Victorian wood carving in the church which is impressive if somewhat gloomy.

The village has mostly C19 cottages lining a straggling main street.

Driffield (Map B1) 4 m. SE of Cirencester

A picture-postcard remote village on a hill overlooking rich farmland. A characteristic group of stone-built, stone-tiled cottages opposite the church is typical of the charming domestic buildings in the area.

Duxford (Photo 22, Map B4) off A420 1 m. N of Hinton Waldrist

East Hagbourne (Photo 23, Map C5) off B4016 1 m. S of Didcot
P.O.|Shop|Pubs

In 1659 the church was unharmed but most of the houses were destroyed by fire. Today, however, the village contains a number of handsome C17/18 houses, built of brick and timber with leaded panes, wooden mullions and windows with elaborate ironwork handles. Modern houses have been added which do not spoil the charm of the long village street. There is a pleasant walk which starts nearly opposite the PO, follows Hacca brook and then turns right to the church.

East Hendred (Photo 24, Map C5) off A417 4 m. E of Wantage
P.O.|Shops|Pubs with food|Fish Farm

The wealth of timber-framed cottages, Tudor brick, thatched and tiled roofs, wooden barns, stone outbuildings and romantic churches and chapels make East Hendred a unique Downland village, which in 1970 was placed under a Conservation Order.

In the Middle Ages the village was an

23 *East Hagbourne— Village Centre. The Norman village cross, with five steps and three sundials, has fine timber-framed buildings on either side. St Andrew's Church (C12/15) has a rare bell-cote (1490). This small stone belfry contains the original sanctus bell rung before each service for 500 years. Sadly the bell-cote is now in urgent need of repair.*

important market and a centre for the rich wool trade. Many of the fine houses in the parish were built before the trade moved to other towns such as Wantage. An interesting place to explore on foot as the many lanes, passages and pathways reveal the treasures of the village.

Hendred House is a late-medieval building with Elizabethan, Georgian and Victorian additions. It is the home of the Eyston family, (descendants of St Thomas More), who have lived here for over 500 years. The private chapel of St Amand (C13) is attached to the house and the Roman Catholic religion has been practised here since 1291.

At the E end of the village is a C15 wayside chapel which now houses a small museum with items of local interest.

St Augustine of Canterbury Church is mainly of Early English origin with a perpendicular tower. The interior was restored in Victorian times. The lectern is particularly interesting as it seems too grand for a small country church. It was made in the C13 for use by both the priest and the leader of the choir and has two book ledges—the lower one for the use of the cantor when on his knees in prayer. The octagonal pulpit is Jacobean with carved foliage with a portrait of Charles on one of the front panels.

Above the village are gallops for racing horses on the Downs and the Ridgeway, and strings of horses can be seen leaving and returning to the stables.

Eastleach Martin and Eastleach Turville (Photo 25, Map A3) 5 m. N of Lechlade
P.O.

The setting of these tiny hamlets between wooded hills is most attractive, particu-

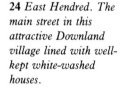

24 *East Hendred. The main street in this attractive Downland village lined with well-kept white-washed houses.*

larly in the spring when masses of daffodils are in bloom beside the River Leach which runs between the two hamlets. It seems probable the hamlets were held by different lords since there are churches in each of the two places only a few hundred yards apart but separated by the river.

There is a pleasant walk from Eastleach to Southrop which follows the river and then returns along a path and lane across the river at each of the villages.

Eaton Hastings (Map B3) off A417 5 m. E of Lechlade

The old village stood by the river but nothing now remains except the church and a few cottages. A field called Town Meadow S of the church has mounds which might be the remains of the medieval houses. One explanation for vanished or shrunken villages is that a pestilence such as the Black Death drove the people away and this may have happened at Eaton Hastings. However it may have been a victim of an early enclosure since the lord of the manor, a member of the Fettiplace family, carried out enclosures in the area, turning out the villagers so that the fields could be used for grazing sheep.

St Michael is a small Norman Church with a Jacobean pulpit and a stained-glass window by Burne-Jones.

A striking figure of an angel in prayer stands on a memorial to the 1st Baron Faringdon (of Buscot) and his wife outside the w end of the church, and a stained- glass window in their memory,

25 *Eastleach—Stone bridge over the River Leach. In the spring the wide bank of daffodils beside the shallow sparkling stream makes a delightful picture. Eastleach Martin church can be seen through the trees. The footbridge of large flat brown stones is known as Keble's Bridge, either after John Keble, the famous C19 churchman, curate here (1815–1818), or after the Keble family who held the manor for five generations in C16.*

26 *Thatchers at Clifton Hampden. The craft of thatching, once in sad decline, is now in great demand and some fine work can be seen in many villages. Long straw (ordinary wheat or rye straw) is not usually available as the combine harvester prefers short-strawed corn. Combed-wheat reed, first used in the W country, lasts for 30 years and Norfolk reed for 60 years or more. They both shed rain well and can be shaped to give the traditional 'tea cosy' look.*

erected by their sons and daughter, is in the W windows.

Ewelme (Map C6) off A423 5. SE of Dorchester

P.O.|Shop|Pubs|Fish Farm|Garage
St Mary's Church Built in the C15 by the Earl and Countess of Suffolk on the site of an older church. The early C14 tower still stands. There are unusual chequer patterns of squared stones and flint on the E end and the embattled parapet is built of bricks, resembling many Suffolk churches. The setting of the church, on a hill, overlooking the village and a valley, is particularly charming. Jerome K. Jerome, author of 'Three Men in a Boat', is buried in the churchyard with his wife and daughter. The beautifully propor-

tioned interior, largely unaltered since the C15 and well lit, gives an impression of grace and dignity, enhanced by the many fine tombs, carvings, brasses and stained glass.

The carved wooden font cover is 10½ ft in height and was the gift of John Duke of Suffolk after the death of his mother Alice in 1475. The figure at the top is St Michael and the counterpoise is carved with a Tudor rose. The canopy fell in 1823 and was then restored. St John's Chapel is as wide as the chancel and the same length. The E window has four large lights of C15 stained glass and the open timber roof has carved angels at the intersections of the beams.

The tomb of Alice, Duchess of Suffolk, and grand-daughter of Geoffrey Chaucer, lies between the chancel and St John's

Chapel, with an alabaster effigy wearing a coronet and robes with the Order of the Garter on the left arm. The tomb has a canopy on which are three sections with carved stone angels, a band of quatrefoils with flower ornaments in the centre. Above these sections are four pinnacles on either side of the canopy surmounted by wooden carved figures of monks and angels.

Thomas and Matilda Chaucer's tomb, parents of Alice, Duchess of Suffolk, in St John's Chapel, is surmounted by the brasses of Thomas in plate armour and his wife in a mantle, veil and wimple. On the sides of the tomb are many medieval shields of arms which were restored in 1843.

From the w door of the church there is a covered passage which leads to the cloister of the *Almshouse* built in 1437 of mellow local red brick. Although the decorative use of brick, creating varied patterns, was often used in East Anglia at that time it is most unusual to find it in Oxfordshire. The square courtyard of the cloister is surrounded by the houses of the Almsmen, originally thirteen but reduced in 1970 to seven. The office of Master of the Almshouse has, from 1605, been united with that of Regius Professor of Medicine at Oxford.

The *School* founded in 1437 adjoins the Almshouse and is mainly Georgian with some C15 brickwork. It is now a Church of England maintained Primary School.

Ewelme is an exceptionally attractive village with a wealth of old buildings set in narrow streets which wind up the hills on which they stand. At various points in the village the flourishing watercress beds can be seen, fed by the stream once known as the 'King's Pool'.

Eynsham (Map A5) on A40 and B4044
5 m. w of Oxford
Market Day—Thurs. | *Parking and Toilets*—town centre. | *Good range of Shops | Pubs with food | Restaurants | Cafés | P.O. | Banks | Garage | Fish Farm*
The town is small and has a pleasant centre with grey-stone cottages and the church standing to one side of The Square. Nothing now remains of the Benedictine Abbey founded in 1005 AD, by Aelfric, a distinguished scholar. At the dissolution in C16 it was the second wealthiest abbey in the county and had extensive fish farms. A modern fish farm, sited on the Church Hanborough road, occupies the old mill and has revived this medieval trade.

St Leonard's Church adjoins The Square, dedicated to St Leonard, patron saint of prisoners, largely C15, restored in 1856 and 1892.

Eynsham is about a mile from the Thames over which is *Swinford Toll Bridge*. The bridge was built by the 4th Earl of Abingdon in 1769, replacing a dangerous ford. The toll is still charged although various attempts to buy the bridge have been made by the local authorities. The owners of the toll are governed by the Act which gave permission for the bridge to be built and this allows the toll to be lowered but not raised. However the wording of the Act, charging per wheel, made it possible in 1955 to raise the charge to take account of the spare wheel. The money taken is free of income tax since builders of bridges were considered, in the C18, to be public benefactors and as such immune from rates and taxes. The bridge is a handsome structure built with a light, creamy stone in an elegant classic style. The approach walls and central balustrade form an unbroken curve and the arches are beautifully graduated. It is best seen from the river bank.

There is a pleasant walk from Eynsham Lock adjoining the bridge, along the towpath towards Wytham Woods.

Fairford (Map B2) on A417 between Cirencester and Lechlade
P.O. | Parking in centre of town | *Good range of Shops | Book-Shop*—Colston House, Market Place | *Toilets | Hotels | Pubs | Restaurants | Cafés | Banks | Garage | Leisure Centre*—Lechlade Rd
St Mary's Church rebuilt in 1490 to 1500 in richest late perpendicular by John Tame and his son Sir Edmund Tame. It is famous for the spectacular twenty-eight stained-glass windows which present in vivid pictures the story of the Bible from the Garden of Eden

27 *Faringdon—Town Hall and* Crown Hotel, *Market Place. The* Crown Hotel *has a Georgian front, with C14 courtyard and an open Jacobean staircase. The most interesting building in the Market Place is the C17 Town Hall, on Tuscan columns with a small open area below.*

28 *Filkins—A fine group of traditional farm buildings converted to a weaving mill, exhibition gallery and shop. A barn, built in 1721, of splendid proportions,*

to the Last Judgment. The glass is probably the work of Barnard Flower, Master Glass Painter to Henry VII and covers an area of 2000 square feet. This complete set of medieval glass in a parish church has been preserved in its original form and is unique in the country. The roof inside the church has notable work in oak, beams supported by carved angels with swords, scrolls, sceptres or shields. The choir stalls are decorated with fourteen misericords depicting everyday life in the time of Henry VII and there are also finely carved screens.

Grey stone houses of the C17/18 stand in the *Market Place*, the larger houses being on the E side. These pleasant dignified houses recall the time when Fairford was a rich wool town and had the advantage of a market. There was also a ford across the Coln which flows through the town, from which Fairford

took its name – 'fair' (easy to cross) ford. The Mill House, in Mill Lane, is a picturesque restored stone building on the Coln.

Faringdon (Photo 27, Map B3) at junction of A417 and A4095
Market Day—Tues. | *Tourist Infm.*— Southampton St (Easter to October) | *Parking*—Market Place and Southampton St | *Toilets*—Southampton St | *P.O.* | good range of usual *Shops*, including a number of antique shops | *Hotels* | *Pubs* | *Restaurants* | *Cafés* | *Banks* | *Garage*
Faringdon was the first capital of all Wessex, commanding the upper reaches of the Thames and the Ridgeway. Although the capital later moved to Winchester Faringdon remained a prominent town in Saxon times with a

royal residence supposed to have been on the site of the *Salutation Inn*, opposite the parish church.

The town has always been important in the area as a market town since it is the natural centre for the farmers of the Vale of the White Horse. Pig farming in the area was particularly successful and large quantities of smoked bacon were produced, to be sent to Oxford and London. Farming still remains the principal industry in the district.

All Saints Church This large cruciform church stands at the top of the Market Place with the trees of Faringdon House behind. Built mostly in the C12/13 in traditional Norman and Early English styles. The w window, a N aisle and a N chancel chapel were built in the C15. The spire was knocked off the C13 tower by cannon fire in the Civil War.

The church is distinguished by ex-ceptionally beautifully carved stone both in the Georgian headstones in the graveyard, on the flowered capitals of the nave arcades and on the four supports of the central tower. There are also several brasses, tombs and memorials of the Untons, Pyes and other notable local families.

Faringdon House is a particularly charming stone house built in 1780, standing on the edge of a ridge looking northward to a private lake, the Upper Thames and the Cotswolds. It is a square house with three stories and a stone attic hidden by a parapet. When it was owned by Lord Berners he built, in 1935, a folly tower 140ft high culminating in a Gothic octagonal lantern, the last folly of any size to be built in England. It stands among Scots pines on the hill known as *Faringdon Folly* on the Oxford side of the town.

formerly known as the Bridal Barn, now houses the Cotswold Woollen Weavers. It contains a working weaving mill, a mill shop selling cloths, garments, rugs and furnishing fabrics. The exhibition gallery shows how wool from the ancient Cotswold breed of sheep is turned into cloth and also gives much information on the history of wool. A coffee shop on the premises serves drinks and snacks. Open Mon.–Sat. 10–6, Sun. 2–6 (no admission charge). Other enterprises such as an Art Gallery are being opened nearby.

29 Filkins—Charming houses in Filkins with fences made of large slabs of stone quarried locally. St Peter's Church (opposite these houses) was built in C19 by G.E. Street in his French Gothic style and is a good example of his excellent work.

In the *Market Place* is the C17 *Town Hall* and a number of C17/18 stone-built houses, some with modern shop fronts. The former Pump House has been converted into a Community Centre.

Filkins (Photos 28, 29, Map A3) off A361 5 m. N of Lechlade
P.O.|Shops|Pubs
The village is an ancient settlement and Anglo-Saxon skeletons and other remains have been found in an area near the present swimming pool. From the tax returns of 1665 it seems probable that Filkins was settled by freemen building their own houses. There are today many very large slabs of stone used as fences and the old lock-up is roofed with them.

Sir Stafford Cripps was a generous benefactor to the village. A Community centre, swimming pool and good stone

council houses were largely paid for by him.

A magnificent C18 barn has now been converted into premises for the Cotswold Woollen Weavers (Photo 28.)

Fyfield (Photo 30, Map B4) off A420 5 m. W of Abingdon
P.O.|Shop|Pub with food|Garage
Fyfield Manor, a handsome and most impressive house with a fine presence, is next to the church. The house was used for various purposes and had fallen into disrepair when the lease was bought by James Parker, an historian and Oxford bookseller. He did much to restore it to its former glory but it again deteriorated until it was bought by Blackwells, the booksellers, whose Rare Books department now occupies the Manor. The house has been completely

restored and is open as a bookshop during normal shop hours. The solar and other large rooms, with handsome beams, are now filled with a wealth of books on a variety of subjects. Fine oak bookcases house rare books, some of which are almost as old as the house itself but the stock also includes modern first editions and beautiful books printed by private presses such as the Whittington Press at Andoversford.

A short walk away from the Manor House is the *White Hart Inn*. This house was built in the C15 for Sir John Golafre who died in 1442. In his will he left money to provide for a chantry priest and five almsmen and the building contained a hall, kitchen and living quarters for the priest. The priest's lower room is now the Dining Room and the kitchen is the Public Bar. Extensive repairs were carried out in 1963: the original proportions of the hall were restored to the full height of the house, and the C15 arch-braced roof was exposed.

When visited the range of the menu offered was wide and the quality of the meals provided of a very high standard.

Godstow (Map A5) off A34 **NW** of Oxford on Thames near Godstow Lock
Pub with food
A nunnery was founded here in 1133 and the church adjoining dedicated in 1139 by King Stephen. The nunnery became a fashionable school for noble girls and Rosamund de Clifford was a pupil there. She later became the mistress of Henry II and when she died in 1176 her body was buried at Godstow. Queen Eleanor is said to have killed her in the nunnery. Her tomb was venerated as a shrine but in 1191 the Bishop of

30 *Fyfield Manor. Built of stone in the C14 by Sir John Golafre, stands near a triangular green. It has Elizabethan additions with mullioned windows and gables. Sir Thomas White, a rich London merchant, and his family owned the house for about 200 years. It then passed into the ownership of St John's College, Oxford, which he founded. Now owned and beautifully restored by Blackwells, it houses their Rare Books Department in a splendid setting.*

Lincoln, disapproving of so much attention to a lady of doubtful virtue, had her remains re-buried outside. It is said that the nuns dug up her coffin again and put it back into their church. After the dissolution by Henry VIII the building became a private house in 1539, was fortified and held for the King, burned in 1645 either by Fairfax or the owner David Walter, and finally destroyed in 1646. Nothing remains except a C15 walled enclosure and the shell of a chapel, in which cows now graze. When Godstow Lock was cut the stone coffins of the nuns were used to make a footpath to nearby Wytham.

The nearby *Trout Inn* adjoins the river, beside the medieval bridge and is a favourite place in the summer for visitors from Oxford. A thunderous lasher with foaming white cascades of water and scores of fish provide entertainment, as do a number of elegant peacocks. The fish, fed by the patrons of the pub, gather in shoals by the terrace. The *Perch Inn* at Binsey can be reached by walking for a mile along the towpath (see Binsey), past the ruins of Godstow Nunnery towards Oxford. Both pubs provide good food.

Great Coxwell (Map B3) off the A420 1½ m. sw of Faringdon
Tithe Barn The finest surviving medieval barn in the country, was built for the Cistercian monks of Beaulieu Abbey in the late C13 to store the produce to which their tithes and rent entitled them. The amount of produce which the barn contained is shown by its immense size—152ft long and 51 ft

31 East Hanney—Post Office. In a 'stone-hungry' area this house built of local brick with a tiled roof shows the good use made of local material to construct attractive buildings. The sub-Post Office, sadly disappearing from many villages, survives here with a village shop.

igh. William Morris considered it to
be 'as noble as a cathedral'. It is built
of stone with a stone-slated roof and air
vents in the walls; the timber roof is
supported on immense oak beams standing on square stone pedestals about six
ft high. Adjoining the barn is a C17
stone farmhouse with a duckpond. The
NT now administers the barn and it can
be visited at most times.

St Giles Church Nave was built in
about 1200: narrow chancel arch in the
C13. The top of the tower is perpendicular with gargoyles in Cotswold stone.
The dark trussed wooden roof of the
nave and the three stained-glass windows
in the chancel are an effective combina-
tion in this small and pleasant building.

Hanney—East and **West** (Photo 31,
Map B4) off A338 3 m. N of Wantage
P.O.|Shop|Pubs with food
The Hanneys are separated by only half
a mile and are similar in character,
having houses of local brick, timber-
frame and thatch and small greens, and
brooks. Houses in both villages are well
maintained and a number occupied by
people working at Harwell.

St James Church in West Hanney has
a C12 tower on the N side, a Norman N
door, a transitional font and several fine
brasses.

There is a causeway of flagstones
starting from the church, passing the
walls of West Hanney House and con-
tinuing towards East Hanney.

Venn Mill on the A338, N of East
Hanney was built in about 1800 and a
mill on the site is mentioned in the
Doomsday Book. Milling stopped about
1941. The building was later used for
other purposes but is now being restored
to a working condition.

Harwell (Photo 32, Map C5) on A4130
3 m. W of Didcot
*P.O.|Shops|Pubs with food|Fruit
Farms|Garage*
The area around Harwell has long been
famous for the fruit grown on the greensand soil and today there are still very
extensive orchards surrounding the
village.

*Atomic Energy Research Establishment
—Harwell.* The AERE was established to
carry out research on the peaceful uses
of atomic energy on a former airfield at
Harwell in 1946 and has since spread
into the adjoining parishes of Chilton
and East Hendred. The effect of the
move of this major industry to Harwell
has been immense since it has caused
large increases in the population and in
money brought into the area. At first
the numbers of people in Abingdon and
Wantage doubled but later the workers
at Harwell spread over other parts of
the county. This injection of mainly
young well-educated people into the
region has effected a large social and
economic gain which has raised the
quality of life in many ways which are
not immediately apparent. The people
of the AERE have enlivened various
clubs and their committees and have
also increased considerably the size of
the church congregations.

St Matthew's Church Mainly C13,
stands on a mound near the Chilbrook
stream which flows through the village.
The size shows that at one time the
population in the area was large enough
to support a building of these proportions
and in 1963 remains of a chancel and
aisleless nave were found. Restored in
1867, it still retains the atmosphere of
its original builders. E window has some
fine decorated tracery and stained glass
with arms of Piers Gaveston, Lord of
the Upper Manor and friend of Edward
II. Other windows contain more C14
stained glass and there are interesting
stone sculptures on the S and N side of
the chancel arch. The rare timbered oak
roofs are mainly original, dating from
the C13. The churchyard is not now used
for burials and the path to the church
is lined with tombstones.

Hatherop (Map A2) off A417 3 m. N of
Fairford
Distinguished by an unusual church—*St
Nicholas*, rebuilt in 1854-5 by Lord de
Mauley. The church has an unmistakable
French look about it, described in 'Build-
ings of England' as Perp cum French-
Gothic. The central tower is in two
stages with a steeply pitched roof and a

32 Harwell. The village contains several large, well-maintained brick and timber houses, tiled, thatched and pargeted, and has an air of prosperity. A number of cottages have been dated by radiocarbon—Le Carillon (about 1425) and Dell Cottage (about 1445) in Church Lane, and School House (about 1600) in Sennings Lane; all of cruck construction.

handsome weathercock. The interior of the church is richly decorated with carved stone friezes showing castles, leaves, flowers and the initial B for Barbara, Lady de Mauley. Her life-like marble statue by Raffaelle Monti (the sculptor of Father Thames at St John's Lock, Lechlade) is in the chapel and like the other work in the church is startling in its perfection of form and high quality of workmanship.

Highworth (Photo 33, Map C3) at junction A361, B4000 and B4019 5 m. NE of Swindon
P.O.|Shops|Banks|Hotel|Restaurants| Pubs with food|Bookshop—High St| Garage|Recreation Centre with outdoor swimming pool

An unspoilt prosperous little town, a very pleasant place to visit. There is parking in the centre and another car park a short walk away. Three great families owned most of the land round Highworth and they brought trade and prosperity to the town enabling bakers, grocers, iron-mongers, harness-makers, shoe-makers and other shops and services to flourish. Today the rich farming land around Highworth still supports a variety of shops and services, unusual in a town of this size, especially as it is near Swindon with its enormous Brunel shopping complex.

There are a number of C18/19 houses of some interest round the square including *Jesmond House Hotel* (early C18), Westrop House (early C19) and Highworth House (early C18), which

faces the churchyard.

St Michael's Church is mostly C13/14 with a Norman tympanum on the s wall showing Samson and the Lion. In the Civil War the church was fortified and held for the King but was captured by the Roundheads under Fairfax. The church tower was hit by a cannon bell near the doorway.

Hinton Waldrist (Map B4) off A420
9 m. **w** of Abingdon
P.O./Shop
Hinton is the Saxon name for a high settlement and Waldrist a corruption of St Valery, the name of the family who held the land in the C12. In Roman times there was a fort called Achester on the site defending the ford at Duxford. Round the Elizabethan Manor are the remains of the moat of the castle of the St Valerys, and a motte to the sw probably belonged to the castle. Sir Henry Marten, one of the signatories of the death warrant of Charles I, lived in the Manor in the C17. It later became the property of the Loders and marble tablets in the church record the deaths of the various members of the Loder and Loder-Symonds families.

The village also contains a number of other attractive stone houses, the gardens of which are often open to the public in the summer.

On the A420 there is a thatched stone tollhouse built in 1733, now restored as a private house.

The Icknield Way came into use after the Ridgeway Path although its name is

33 Highworth—Sheep St. A street of C17/18 shops, pub and Post Office adjoining the Market Place, typical of the many well-kept and attractive buildings in the town.

34 *Iffley Lock. One of the locks on the Thames near Oxford, with gay borders of flowers. One of Salter's steamers which, in the summer, run between Oxford and Abingdon is in the lock. There was a pound lock here in 1632 (one of the first three locks on the Thames). The original lock is now used as a weir, as is the mill-race of a former mill destroyed by fire in 1908.*

lost in history, having no traceable etymological source. It follows the spring-line where water was available to travellers and provided a route between settlements. Although a very ancient route, it was used when there was less danger from animals in the woods, some of which had been cleared. Parts of the Icknield Way became Roman roads because the Romans too needed water on the march and it provided a route between their towns.

Today, in the area covered by this book, a section of the Way is a metalled road—B4507, w of Wantage. E of Wantage the Way is shown on the OS map as a public path as far as Hagbourne Hill. From this point there are different possible routes for its continuation, part of the A417 being shown as the Icknield Way.

Iffley (Photo 34, Map B5) off A4158
2 m. SE of centre of Oxford
P.O.│Hotel│Pubs
St Mary the Virgin Church Built about 1170–80 in the elaborate late C12 style. Is considered to be the finest unspoiled example of a Norman church in the country. The sculpture of the windows and doorways is without equal in its elaborate decoration and natural detail. The chancel, central tower and aisleless nave remain as they were built and Victorian restorations were carried out with taste and care. At the S entrance to the church is an ancient yew tree said to be as old as the church. The S doorway has rose mouldings, and fantastic beasts. Above are zig-zag and sawtooth decorations with knights on horseback and centaurs. The w doorway is the most magnificent, deeply recessed and lavishly

ornamented. It was probably used for entry on ceremonial occasions and has four arches richly decorated with zig-zag moulding and two twisted columns ornamented with 110 beakheads.

Inside the church the square font, large enough for the total immersion of infants, is supported by three C12 spiral columns and one of the C13.

The Rectory near the church was also built in the C12/13 with C16 alterations and is an attractive gabled stone building with brick chimney stacks and a red-tiled roof. The village is largely unspoilt with many stone-built houses of good quality which have been carefully preserved.

Iffley Lock is reached by a short walk down Mill Lane.

Inglesham Church (Photo 35, Map B3) off A361 1 m. **s** of Lechlade

The road leading to the church is narrow but parking is available outside the church.

St John Baptist Church A tiny C13 church of considerable charm, once a priory chapel: the farmhouse adjoining was originally the priory. Although it was restored in 1888–9 by the Society for the Protection of Churches this was done so well that the church still retains the character and atmosphere of the C13. The Jacobean box pews with special pews for squire and vicar are intact, there is an Elizabethan pulpit and interesting sculptures including an unusual Saxon wall-carving of the Virgin and Child showing the bodies in profile but the heads full face. A brass plaque near the **s** door records that 'This Church was repaired in 1888/9 through the energy and with the help of William Morris who loved it'. Kelmscott, a few

35 Inglesham—St John Baptist Church. A visit to this church is highly recommended—it is an unspoilt gem in a solitary peaceful setting. When visited the church was decorated for Harvest Festival, flowers and fruit were displayed throughout and the brass William Morris plaque was highly polished. Obviously local people still love and care for this unusual building.

miles down the river, was the home of Morris. The church is now in the care of the Redundant Churches Fund.

Kelmscott (Map B3) off B4449 3 m. E of Lechlade
Pub with meals and accommodation
A small remote village by the Thames, famous as the holiday home of William Morris, author, poet, artist, craftsman, decorator, printer and reformer. Morris lived here for twenty-five years from 1871 and on his death in 1896 he was buried in the graveyard of the local church, St George. His daughter, May Morris, kept the house open to visitors until 1938. It is now owned by the Society of Antiquaries and is open from 11-1 and 2-5 on the first Wed. of each month from April to September, or by appointment. The house is now well looked after and many of the tapestries, carpets, wallpapers and paintings of Morris can be seen. Rossetti, who lived in the house for a time, and was said to have been in love with Morris's wife, Jane, painted her portrait in a blue silk dress and this also is on view.

St George is a small cruciform church mostly Norman with later additions. There is a C13 gabled bellcote. The tomb of Morris, designed by Philip Webb, is similar to a Viking ridged tomb-house and has badly weathered lettering.

Kemble (Map B1) on A429 4 m. SW of Cirencester
Pub with food | Railway station (service to London)—elliptical-arch bridges built by I.K. Brunel
Quiet village with an Early English church, rebuilt in the C19. Kemble House is a C17 stone manor house. On the A429 ½ m. N of Kemble the stripling River Thames can be seen from the road by parking near the remains of railway embankments. This is the first road bridge over the river where running water can always be seen. The shallow rippling stream is a charming sight when covered by a flowering blanket of water-crowfoot in June (see Frontispiece).

Smerrill Farm Museum is between Cirencester and Kemble on the A429. It is open daily from 10.30-6.00. The museum has a unique private collection of bygones from the Man and Horse era.

Kempsford (Map B2) off A417 3 m. S of Fairford
P.O. | Pub
Once an important place as a ford of the Thames, was defended by a Saxon and later by a Norman castle. John of Gaunt who owned the castle married Blanche of Kempsford, a descendant of the Duke of Lancaster and a patroness of Chaucer. John built the great tower of the church between 1385 and 1399. The castle was demolished, replaced in Jacobean times, destroyed again in 1790 and replaced by the present Manor Farmhouse.

St Mary's Church with its handsome tower stands above the river. It has a Norman nave with four original deeply splayed windows, a fine timber roof, choir stalls excellently designed by G.E. Street with fanned leaves on the ends and heraldic paintings in the tower vaulting.

The Thames and Severn Canal, opened in 1789, once ran through the village and a Wharf House still remains. Although the Thames can be seen from the churchyard there is no public right of way to the river from the village.

Kingston Bagpuize and Southmoor (Map B4) at junction of A415 and A420 6 m. W of Abingdon
P.O. | Shop | Pubs with food | Fruit Farms | Garage
Kingston House A fine house built in the 1st quarter of the C17 of red brick with Cotswold stone dressings in the style of Wren and Vanbrugh, possibly by George Townsend of Bristol, with panelled rooms, a magnificent cantilevered staircase, a Rococo chimney-piece and period furniture. The gardens are large and contain beautiful trees, lawns, woodlands and herbaceous borders. House and gardens are open to the public at various times in the summer.

St John the Baptist Church Built in 1799 of light coloured brick in the Italian Renaissance style. Has a cupola with wooden columns over the w door. Two imitation Norman windows were inserted by E. Dolby of Abingdon in 1882 and are much criticised in guide books.

The two villages were brought together in one parish in 1971 after new housing developments linked them. There is now heavy traffic on the A420 passing through the villages. Kingston is Saxon in origin having been a King's Fort in that time, and a Norman Knight, Ralph de Bachepuise, owned the manor after the conquest, giving his name to the village.

Kingston Lisle (Map C4) off B4507
6 m. w of Wantage
P.O.|Pub with food|Forge

Approached from Wantage, the road runs through a mile-long avenue of tall beech trees which show the beauty of the shape and colour of these magnificent trees.

The village was once owned by the de Lisles who in 1336 created a park covering 300 acres. From the late C14 the property passed through various hands. A house was built in the C18, with wings added in 1812. The architect of the house is not known but it contains a unique flying staircase of a most unusual design. A collection of fine furniture, glass, needlework and carpets made in William Morris designs can be seen. *Kingston Lisle House* is open to the public at various times in the summer.

The park and gardens are now landscaped, the house overlooking a valley with narrow lakes overhung by trees. The s front of the house has immacu-

36 *Langford. St Matthew's Church is one of the finest surviving Anglo-Saxon churches in England with a tower built in about 1040 of noble proportions. The N wall of the nave has two flying buttresses erected in 1574. Inside the church there is a pulpit made in 1673, a C15 font and modern painted panels.*

37 *Lechlade—Canal Round House and Warehouse. Near Lechlade, the Thames and Severn Canal meets the Thames. Round houses built for lock-keepers and lengthmen have three rooms, one above the other, with a spiral staircase built into the thickened wall on one side holding the fireplace and flues. The Coln flows into the Thames near the round house. The best approach is by a track off the A417, 1/2 m. W of Lechlade.*

lately clipped yews, and round the house are some imposing tall cedars.

Church of St John the Baptist opposite the lodge of the house is of Norman origin with roughcast walls, a wooden bell-turret and small spire. Some outstanding carving on the pew-ends, pulpit and screen of the C17. C14 murals on the N wall depicting scenes from the story of St John the Baptist are probably the finest examples of this period to be seen in any parish church in the whole country.

Up the hill S of the village is a *Blowing Stone*, in front of a cottage garden. It is a brown sarsen stone about 3½ ft high with holes which when blown through are said to have trumpeted a warning to the neighbourhood in the time of King Alfred the Great.

Langford (Photo 36, Map B3) off A361 3½ m. NE of Lechlade
P.O.|Shop|Pubs with food
Langford, Broadwell, Kencot, Filkins and Broughton Poggs are five villages in the Upper Thames Valley which have remained unspoilt by the industrial revolution. They are surrounded by rich farming land, well watered by streams running into the Thames. Limestone, easily available, was used for building the churches, the manors and farm houses, the cottages and the dry-stone walls. Today the villages, mostly no longer occupied by farm workers, are well maintained and have an air of prosperity. Small local industries are coming into the area such as the group of restored farm buildings at Filkins. The roar of jet planes from

RAF Brize Norton is the only disturbance of the rural peace.

St Matthew's Church The greatest treasures of the church are the stone carvings of the Crucifixion with Figures and the Langford Rood re-set in the C13 S porch. The Crucifix and the figures of Our Lady and St John have been re-set and the frame altered and partly renewed. The arms of Christ have been transposed so that they are now inclined downwards and hands reversed. The figures have been transposed because they now look away from the cross. In the tradition of the early church Christ is shown as a suffering human being rather than as a divine figure whom pain could not touch.

The Langford Rood showing Christ in a long robe is on the outside E wall of the S porch and is a unique sculpture in limestone. The head is missing and would not now fit into the space provided above the figure.

There is a typescript available in the church which is a well-written and forth-right description of the church and its many treasures. It contains an excellent account of the building including the statement that 'Anglo-Saxon mortar was very good and greatly superior to Norman mortar'.

Lechlade (Photos 37, front and back covers, Map B3) at junction of A361 and A417
Parking—Centre of town | *Toilets*—Burford St. | *P.O.* | *Banks* | *Garage* | *Garden Centre* | *Bookshop*—Oak St | *Shopping*—good variety | *Sailing Club* | *Hotels* | *Pubs with food/Restaurant* | *Cafés* | *Caravan Park*—St John's Priory, A417 | *Camping Park*—Bridge House, A361 | *Boats for hire* at riverside, also petrol, diesel and calor gas.
Parking and picnic site on A361 ½ m. S of town centre give access to a long stretch of the Thames, making it possible to drive a car quite near to the river. The picnic site is well maintained with a very large area of mown grass and trees for shade. The town is a short distance away reached by walking over Halfpenny Bridge. There are toilets by the car park.

The town takes its name from the small tributary of the Thames called Leach or Lech which flows into the river to the SE. Lechlade is a beautiful town mostly stone-built with many handsome substantial C17/19 houses. Richard Pace, a local architect, built many houses here in the C19 using both the golden Cotswold and the grey Oxfordshire stone.

Halfpenny Bridge built in 1792 was, as its name suggests, a toll-bridge: a toll-house still stands beside it.

For over a thousand years Lechlade was a considerable trading centre and in 1789 a canal extended the navigation to the Severn. There is no longer a fair nor a market at Lechlade but until river and canal traffic declined there were busy wharfs at the riverside where boats were loaded with the products of the countryside including large quantities of cheese and other dairy products.

A stone figure of Father Thames, by R Monti, made for the Crystal Palace Exhibition of 1851, is now at *St John's Lock*, the highest lock on the Thames. It was first placed at Thames Head, Trewsbury Mead, but was removed in 1974 because of vandalism. *St John's Bridge* by the side of the lock was rebuilt in stone in 1299, pulled down and again rebuilt in 1884.

St Lawrence Church, one of the great Gloucestershire 'wool' churches, is wholly perpendicular, built in 1476 in Taynton stone. St Lawrence was a Spanish saint and the church was re-dedicated in his name when owned by Katharine of Aragon in the early C16. 'Stanzas in a Summer Evening Church-yard' were written in 1815 by Shelley when he was on a rowing excursion with Mary Godwin, Peacock and Charles Clairmont. Lines from the poem are inscribed on a stone in the churchyard. The spire of the church, a prominent landmark, can be seen for miles around.

Little Faringdon Mill on the River Leach on the A361, listed in the Dooms-day Book, is still in use with its C19 machinery. It has ten 'open days' a year when people may see the mill working. Adjoining the mill is a trout farm where freshwater fish may be caught and bought.

38 *Wittenham Clumps, an ancient Iron Age fort, commands an extensive view of Day's Lock, the river and the surrounding countryside. The original trees on the top of the hill, planted in the late C18, have had to be replaced with new trees and the clump has not yet regained its former size.*

Little Wittenham (Photos 38, 39 Map B6) off A415 6m. SE of Abingdon
The village is above the Thames, near Day's Lock, underneath Wittenham Clumps, one of the Sinodun Hills (a pre-English name for early Iron Age hill forts). There are only a few houses in the village, many half-timbered.

St Peter's Church was rebuilt in 1863 in the Early English style and has a sandstone tower. Inside the church there is a marble and alabaster memorial to a member of the Dunch family with reclining figures and seven kneeling children below.

There is space for car parking outside the church and from here there is a well-trodden footpath to the top of Wittenham Clumps. Other footpaths from Little Wittenham go to Dorchester, Shillingford and Brightwell, the most

popular being a walk of about 1½ m. past Day's Lock across the river meadow to Dorchester, passing Dyke Hills, a pre-Roman Iron Age defended site.

The other ancient hill fort in the area is *Castle Hill* where the deep ditch and outer bank of the Iron Age fortifications are clearly visible. There is a car park below the hill, reached by taking the back road S from Little Wittenham towards Brightwell. Castle Hill was probably built at the same time as Uffington Castle, above the White Horse. Its position and height, commanding views over the river valley as far as the Downs made it an important military camp. Although there are signs of Roman occupation it seems likely that the Romans made little use of it as a military site since the local tribes were quickly pacified, but it may have been used for religious rites. Unfortunately no excavation has been carried out on either of the hills.

Long Wittenham (Map B6) off A415
5 m. SE of Abingdon
P.O.|Shop|Pubs with food
The long main road through the village has many half-timbered brick and plaster houses carefully restored, and these give a pleasing irregular line to the street. A fire in 1868 destroyed many houses and the rebuilding that took place is not quite in keeping with the older buildings. Many of the houses have gardens which run down to a backwater which was once the main stream of the Thames— now running through Clifton Cut. There is a pleasant walk by the side of the Thames of about 1½ m. to Appleford, which starts from Gifford's Lane near the Pendon Museum.

Pendon Museum of Landscape and Transport in Miniature is open from March to October on Sat. Sun. and Bank Holidays from 2–6 p.m., from November to February on Sat. and Sun. from 2–5 p.m. This world-famous museum contains a unique record of building styles in miniature models of cottages, farms, fields, lanes and trains of the 1920s and 1930s. John Ahern's Madder Valley layout and transport relics can also be seen.

St Mary's Church was built, on the site of a wooden Saxon church, of stone brought from Caen in about 1120 by the 3rd Earl of Buckingham who was lord of the manor. The name of the village comes from 'Witta' a Saxon who settled here—hence 'Witta's Ham'. It contains many later additions including a curious memorial to the Earl of Gloucester who died in 1295. This is an effigy of a cross-legged knight only two

39 *View from Little Wittenham Church. Day's Lock and weir are in the foreground, with the village and church of Dorchester on Thames seen in the background.*

ft in length which is said to cover the heart of a C13 knight. There are two sculptured angels on the arch above.

The C12 lead font, concealed during the Civil War by a wooden covering so that it would not be used for bullets, was not removed until 1839 when a table was made from the wood. After the First World War a Roll of Honour with the names of the servicemen who had been killed was placed on it.

Milton (Map C5) off A34 4 m. s of Abingdon
P.O. | *Shop* | *Pub with food*
Milton is the site of an old settlement and was once a centre of the rich wool trade. The *Church of St Blaise*, dedicated to the patron saint of woolcombers, has a C14 tower and porch, the remainder

mostly C19. In the graveyard there are some fine examples of carved tombstones made by local stone-masons who worked for generations in the village.

The church, the *Admiral Benbow* pub and Manor are grouped together off the main road in a pleasant rural setting. From the village there is an interesting walk to the neighbouring village of Steventon (see **Steventon**).

The centre part of *Milton Manor* was built in 1663 in Inigo Jones style and is a simple three-storied red-brick house with all four elevations equal. One of the features of the building is that the front and back of the house are exactly the same and the rooms are also identical in size. The grand oak staircase is over 90 ft high. The wings of the house were built in 1764 when the stables and the walled and landscaped gardens with serpentine lakes were added.

The Calton family owned the Manor until 1764 when it was sold to John Bryant Barrett, a London lace-maker who restored the house. On the first floor a Roman Catholic chapel was created and this contains some fine C13/14 stained-glass from Steventon church and rare Flemish glass of the C17/18. The chapel has the altar facing w, and is decorated in extravagant Strawberry Hill Gothick style, as is the library, which contains few books but a large collection of china, portraits and other memorabilia. The present owner, Mrs Mockler, is a descendant of John Bryant Barrett and usually shows visitors round the house which is open at weekends between Easter and mid-October from 2–5.30 p.m.

Newbridge (Photo 40, Map B4) on A415 2 m. N of Kingston Bagpuize. Newbridge was probably first built in 1250 to provide a passage for the wool traders of Witney whose packhorses must have used it to reach the dry land of the Vale of the White Horse. It crosses the flood plain of the Thames and the Windrush at the narrowest point. Despite its name the bridge is one of the oldest on the river although the method of building the arches shows an advance on Radcot Bridge built about fifty years previously. The spans of the arches are less pointed and the largest is eighteen ft wide so that the roadway is less steeply humped than at Radcot. There are also pedestrian refuges on the bridge on top of cutwaters which give good support. The quality of building probably accounts for the fine condition of all the six original arches, built of Taynton stone brought down the river Windrush, which flows into the Thames at this point. Taynton quarry, near Burford, has for centuries supplied first-class stone to build bridges over the Thames, Oxford colleges, Windsor Castle and to rebuild London after the Great Fire. The quarry was owned by Thomas Strong, one of Wren's master masons, and nearby Upton Quarry by Christopher Kempster who built the County Hall at Abingdon.

Northmoor (Map B4) off A415 8 m. SE of Witney
Pub | Nursery Garden
The Barons of More gave their name to the village when they were lords of the manor between C11 and C13. *St. Denys Church* was built during this period probably by the Abbey of St Denys in Paris which was then connected with Abingdon Abbey. St John's College, Oxford, acquired the property in 1555 and the arms of the college are on either side of the altar. The beautiful carved altar rails, now unfortunately painted in a violent blue colour, were given to St. John's by Archbishop Laud in the C17. The link between Northmoor and St John's still continues.

Rectory Farm adjoining the church is a beautiful Elizabethan house bearing a date-stone of 1588 but probably built before this time. Mr Patrick Florey, whose family has lived in the area since C17, owns the house. The road through the village at one time passed between the church and Rectory Farm and still exists as a grassy track.

The church and the house have a tranquil air, set in the lush Thames countryside with an unchanged beauty as if time had stood still for many centuries.

Nuneham Courtenay (Photo 41, Map B6) on A423 5 m. SE of Oxford
P.O. | Pub with food | Nuneham Nurseries in Nuneham Park—*Mattocks Rose Nurseries*, Clifton Lane | *Garage*
The village was originally called Newnham but was changed to Nuneham Courtenay when the Harcourt family moved there. In planning the classical landscape to be seen from the mansion the 1st Earl Harcourt demolished the entire village and built houses for the villagers on the main Oxford-Henley road, well away from the park. The architect of the new house in the park was Stiff Leadbitter of Eton but his dull plan was greatly altered by subsequent designers. The park with the beautiful view across the Thames which first attracted the Harcourts is occasionally open to the public.

Nuneham Courtenay Arboretum, owned by Oxford University, provides material

or teaching and research, which for reasons of space and soil cannot be provided in the Botanic Garden in Oxford. 0'acres with unusual (in Oxon) acid greensand soil allows cultivation of lime-hating plants such as rhododendrons, azaleas, heathers, camellias and certain rare Chilean shrubs. Entrance about 200 yards E of village, open free in the summer, including Sunday p.m.

Carfax Conduit which now stands in the park overlooking the river once provided spring water for Oxford replacing foul and evil-smelling well water. Otho Nicholson, a Christ Church lawyer, in 1616 paid £2,500 for water to be piped from springs on North Hinksey Hill. A London plumber, Hugh Justyce, constructed a lead cistern containing 20,000 gallons, set in a stone chamber on the hillside, and led the water to Carfax through lead pipes and hollow elm trunks. At Carfax it entered two great cisterns, the upper for the University and the lower, fed by the overflow from the top cistern, for the Town. One cock was provided for the University and one for the Town. John Clark, a Yorkshire carver, embellished the Conduit with a wide variety of images, coats of arms, sundials, mermaids, lettering showing the benefactor's initials (O.N.O.N.) and an Ox from whose pizzle the water came.

In 1694 a pumping station was built to take water from the Thames and this water replaced the supply from the Conduit which had become inadequate for a rising population. However, even after the Conduit was removed, water from the Hinksey pipes was still used until 1868.

All Saints Church (1764) on a hill in the park is a domed building in classical style intended as an ornament to the landscape and not primarily for use as a church.

The other *All Saints Church* in the village is an aisleless church: built in C13 style in 1872 by Edward Harcourt to provide a place of worship for the villagers who disliked the cheerless 'temple' in the distant park.

Oaksey (Map B1) off A429 8 m. S of Cirencester
Pub with food|Farrier
A small village with one street containing

thatched cottages, a forge and *All Saints Church*.

The church has C13 arches and fine Perpendicular clerestory windows and porch. There are a number of gargoyles on the tower and many stone faces on the walls of the nave and chancel arch. The wall paintings are particularly striking and rich in colour, some showing fragments of texts and others showing 'The Christ of Trades'. Christ is surrounded by tools, suggesting that salvation is achieved by work—a moral given in 'Piers Plowman', written shortly before the paintings were done in the early C15. There is also a painting of St Christopher holding a light. A mermaid, fishes swimming and a basket with fish are clearly seen. In the N window there is some excellent C15 stained glass with whole figures of St Anne teaching the Virgin Mary to read and St Catherine crowned.

Oxford
Unfortunately there is not room to include a full guide to Oxford and a short entry would be of little value. There are already many guides to the city available in bookshops and information centres. *The Oxford Information Centre* in St Aldates has a wide range of guide books, maps, postcards and other material. Guided tours of the city also start from the centre.

Purton (Photo 42, Map C2) on B4041 4 m. NW of Swindon
P.O.|Shops|Pubs with food|Garages
An ancient settlement, with Ringsbury Camp occupied in the Iron Age on the W edge of the village. It was a Roman fort and a Saxon town when 'Peartree Village' was turned into Purton. In 1086 the Doomsday Book listed a mill, a wood three miles square, sixty acres of meadow and many acres of ploughland.

The village is now about a mile from the church, probably removed because of plague or fire. High St contains many interesting and handsome houses, among them the former home of the Earl of Clarendon, called College Farm, which

41 *Nuneham Courtenay, Carfax Conduit. When first erected at Carfax in Oxford it was a brilliant, striking monument, built of fine polished stone, painted and gilded in an exuberant gothic style. Although the paint and gilding have gone it is still an impressive piece. It was presented to Lord Harcourt in 1786 when it became a hindrance to traffic. Two inscriptions explaining the reason for the removal were placed on the Conduit, one in Latin for the University and one in English for the Town. Suggestions have been made that the Conduit should now be returned to Oxford and there is no doubt that it should be found a place within the city, if only to revive the custom of making the taps flow with wine on festive occasions.*

42 *Purton. The Manor House is w of the church and was built in about 1600. The aromatic clipped box trees set in a small lawn outside the house complement the symmetry of this lovely building. At the side of the Manor there is a very large L-shaped barn, also of the C17.*

was built in the C16.

St Mary's Church is in a beautiful setting with a perfect C17 manor house and a thatched cottage nearby. An avenue of clipped box with a path of small stones leads to the church. The two towers, both of the same height, one with a steeple make St Mary's unique among English churches. The nave was rebuilt in the C13, the Lady Chapel, central spire, N and S transepts in the C14. In the C15 there was a major rebuilding, three feet being added to the height of the pillars, the N and S aisles rebuilt, the S porch added the W tower erected.

The interior contains many beautiful ancient wall paintings including, in the Lady Chapel, a C14 'Falling Asleep of the Blessed Virgin'. Other wall paintings, including decorations on the arches and above the pillars, have also been restored, and this work continues. In 1872 the church was restored when the box pews

were replaced by pitch pine and the galleries were removed.

Pusey (Map B4) on B4508 10 m. W of Abingdon

Pusey House built of limestone in 1748, probably to the design of John Wood of Bath, has on the garden side a large central block with lower projecting wings. The Pusey family date back, according to legend, to King Canute who presented them with a horn (now in the Victoria and Albert Museum) to be blown in times of invasion—a land tenure system known as 'Cornage'. When the Pusey line became extinct the house and lands passed to the Bouverie-Puseys, one of whom was the Rev Dr Edward Bouverie-Pusey, a member of the Oxford Movement. The present owners are Mr & Mrs Michael Hornby who have re-designed the estate and replanted the gardens in consultation with Geoffrey Jellicoe.

The gardens are now among the finest in England, covering fifteen acres, with fine herbaceous borders, rose gardens, shrubbery, water gardens, magnificent trees, and a view over the lake towards the Downs. The lake is crossed by a Chinese bridge and is well stocked with water-lilies and other aquatic plants. A guide to the gardens contains a Botanical Guide which lists all the varieties of plants to be seen, many of which can be bought near the entrance.

All Saints Church, a small Italianate style building is approached through the grounds of the house or from the lane signed 'village only' to the s of the grounds. It was built in 1745 and the tower in about 1845. Elegant classical arches and beautiful Venetian screens inside the church create a serene atmosphere.

The village with limestone houses and farms is surrounded by well established trees some of which give shade to a rectangular green E of the church—a very good place for a picnic.

Pusey House Gardens are open to the public April to June, Wed. Thurs. Sun., July to mid-October daily (not Mon. Fri) 2–6 p.m.

Quenington (Map A2) off A417 2½ m. N of Fairford
P.O.|Shop|Pubs with food
The village is on the side of a hill running down to the Coln river and has many stone-built houses and dry-stone walls. Quenington Court grounds contain the gatehouse and dovecote of the community of Knights Hospitallers founded in 1193.

St Swithin's Church (C12), restored in a drastic manner in 1882, is distinguished by two exceptionally fine

43 *Radcot Bridge over a Thames backwater.*

Norman doorways which have a great wealth of vigorous carving showing biblical stories as well as rich patterns. The graveyard of the church has been 'tidied' in the same manner as the interior of the church. All the gravestones have been removed to the side wall and the front of the church now resembles a municipal park.

There are pleasant walks along the valley of the Coln from the centre of the village.

Radcot Bridge (Photo 43, Map B3) on A4095 3 m. N of Faringdon
Pub with food | Caravan and camping site | Narrow boat cruises
Radcot Bridge with three arches, now over a backwater, was built before 1312, probably the oldest bridge crossing the Thames and certainly the site of an even older bridge of about 958. The two outside arches may well have been constructed by monks from Beaulieu Abbey who at that time were the only people who knew how to put up the pointed arches and stone ribs similar to those in a church roof. The centre arch was, no doubt, of the same design but was destroyed in 1387 during the war waged between Richard II and Henry Bolingbroke when the battle of Radcot was fought. In 1393 the arch was repaired by fixing a timber framework which was removed when the stone was in position. The middle arch built by this new method was not as strong as the 'church arches' as it shows signs of having been strengthened with tie rods.

During the Civil War, when Radcot was an important defensive outpost for Oxford, then held by the Royalists, there were battles again for the possesion of the bridge.

For centuries, when the Thames was an important highway, river ports such as Radcot were used to load barges taking stone, cheese and other products to London and remains of wharves can still be seen. However by 1871 when May Morris (daughter of William Morris and living at Kelmscott) discovered the bridge it was in a sorry state. The bridge was eventually restored in 1914 but the niche in which a figure of the Virgin Mary stood is still empty.

The bridge now in use over the present navigable channel was built in 1787 because the Thames & Severn Canal Co. said that the centre arch of the old bridge was too narrow for barges.

The Ridgeway (Photo 44) was one of the oldest roads in Europe stretching from the Bristol Channel to a crossing of the Thames at Goring and beyond. There is still a track, maintained by the Countryside Commission, from Overton Hill, near Avebury, to Ivinghoe Beacon in Bucks. The other parts of the Ridgeway have mostly disappeared or have been overlaid by modern roads.

Enough of the road remains to enable us to understand why people from the times of the Stone Age used this route which ran in open country away from the dangers of the wooded and well-watered valley below. Today the track has no villages on it and can be travelled for miles without seeing any signs of human habitation. Near Wayland's Smithy the sky and the land meet on the horizon without interruption—a real horizon, uncluttered by buildings. The Ridgeway is still a highway and as such is open to wheeled vehicles as well as walkers. However, although it is used by farm tractors there are fortunately few cars which can travel along it.

Wayland's Smithy (Photo 44, Map C3) is an ancient burial tomb situated just off the Ridgeway on an impressive site overlooking the Vale. It is not surprising that legends have grown up around the barrow. The Saxons called the site 'Welandes Smidtham', Wayland being a mythical blacksmith who may have shod the White Horse. In the C18 it

was said that if a traveller whose horse had lost a shoe left money and the horse by the Smithy it would be shod by Wayland. Sir Walter Scott embellished this legend in 'Kenilworth'.

A mile E of Wayland's Smithy is the site of *Uffington Castle, White Horse Hill* (858 ft high) the *Manger* and *Dragon Hill* (Map C3).

Uffington Castle covered eight acres surrounded by a bank and ditch which still remain. The castle was an Iron Age hill fort, one of the line of forts stretching along the chalk downs. Below the castle is a conical hill with a flat top called *Dragon Hill*, where tradition has it that St George killed the Dragon, and below is the *Manger*, a deep hollow with curved sides.

Whitehorse Hill, climbed by a narrow road, has a car park near the *White Horse*. This spectacular figure, cut into the white chalk, is 360ft long and 160ft high, and can be seen at a distance from the B4507 near Uffington. The Dept of the Environment says that the figure was probably cut in the C1 AD by a non-Belgic tribe called the Dobunni. A silver coin of the Dobunni was found in Uffington Castle with a horse on it and it was assumed that a horse was their tribal emblem. This is disputed by other experts who consider the horse figure to be very much older. Yet another theory is that King Alfred (around these parts practically anything of interest is attributed to him) was responsible for cutting the figure. The turf outline is regularly cut or scored to keep the outline neat and there is no doubt that the shape, now remarkably modern, has changed over the centuries. White Horse Hill is now in the care of the NT.

Sandford on Thames (Map B5) off A423 3 m. SE of Oxford
P.O.|Pubs with food|Temple Farm Country Club—Caravan and tent pitches
The tall ungraceful chimney of *Sandford Paper Mill* was a landmark for river travellers for many years but the Mill was closed in 1982, ending an industry in the building which started in 1816. There was a mill at Sandford in the C13 when it milled corn—it was rebuilt over

44 *The Ridgeway. Wayland's Smithy, E of Ashbury, is a tomb of great antiquity probably built about 2,820 BC, nearly 1,000 years older than the earliest parts of Stonehenge. This truly immense burial chamber (or barrow) has large stones called Sarsens which supported the walls and now stand at the entrance. These imposing stones were left behind by the Ice Age and are so alien to the chalk Downland that medieval men called them after the Saracens who at the time of the Crusades seemed to be possessed of magical powers. They even thought that the stones grew and perhaps moved of their own accord. For many centuries the barrow was probably used as a burial place for the chiefs of the tribes who ruled over the Vale—a thousand years before the Greeks were civilised. When the barrow was built it was six feet high covered in chalk rubble sloping to the open landscape on the N side so that the white of the chalk was visible for miles around. The grove of trees which now surrounds the mound was planted in the C18.*

45 *Shilton—The Font in Holy Rood Church. The square C14 font was beautifully decorated for Harvest Festival when visited. Carvings from the Passion are on the sides and evangelists at the corners, carried out in a rustic manner. There are also wall-paintings, probably C13 on the s arcade and stone and marble monuments.*

ten years ago after a disastrous fire. The chimney and other buildings were de-molished in 1984 for a housing development.

Sandford Lock Deepest lock on the Thames (8′9″). 1st lock built in 1630s; another built in 1836 when original chamber was used by the mill; rebuilt in 1972/3 including the use of a system bringing in water under the bottom of the lock to reduce turbulence. Sandford is the first lock on the Thames to use this new system.

Kings Arms beside the mill and the lock is a pleasant riverside pub with gardens. The '*Sandford Lashers*', a large weir on a backwater, provides a spectacular sight when the river is high and is a favourite spot for anglers. The lower reaches of the backwater are a popular

spot for swimmers in the summer but the area of the lasher itself is highly dangerous. A memorial stone near the weir commemorates the death by drowning of two friends of J.M. Barrie in 1921, another stone obelisk is in memory of three other undergraduates who also died in the pool.

St Andrew's Church The E and S walls of the chancel are nearly all that remains of the early Norman church built at the end of the C11. it was heavily restored in Victorian times, including the 'Norman style' W tower.

Shilton (Photo 45, Map A3) off A361
8 m. NE of Lechlade
P.O. | *Pub with food*
An attractive stone-built village set

among small hills on which the church and some cottages stand. In the middle of the village there is a shallow ford across the Shill Brook through which cars can be driven.

A steep walk leads to the *Holy Rood Church*, built in 1150 with later additions and restored in 1884/5.

Shrivenham (Map C3) at junction A420, B4000, B4508 6 m. NE of Swindon
P.O.|Shops|Banks|Garages|Pubs with food
Once a small market town, increased in importance first by the Wiltshire and Berkshire Canal in 1810, then by the GWR in 1840. Both the canal and the station have disappeared and the Royal Military College of Science which moved here in 1947 now dominates the town, having taken over Beckett Hall and the estate with its woods and lake. During the war there were many thousands of American troops near Shrivenham and in 1945 the United States Forces University in Europe was based in Beckett Hall.

The main street is wide with many trees, lined with good stone buildings and a number of shops. At present the traffic in the town is heavy but a bypass is under construction and this will greatly improve conditions in the town.
St. Andrew's Church, approached through an avenue of trees and a lych gate, is surrounded by a group of pleasant cottages. Largely rebuilt in 1638, it has a marble C12 font, panelled walls and monuments to the Barrington family who once owned Beckett Hall.

Somerford Keynes (Map B1) 5 m. S of Cirencester
P.O.|Pub|Keynes Park Country Park
The Thames near Somerford Keynes is no more than a stream although until the C19 there was a water mill on the river and a farm here is called Upper Mill Farm. Gravel extraction has been extensive in the area and the village is now surrounded by large lakes. Two lakes to the E have been turned into *Keynes Park Country Park* where fishing, windsurfing, sailing and picnicking can

be enjoyed. The Park also has a nature reserve, a children's playground and an area for barbecues.

Near the church there is a manor house, partly C15/16, and several other large houses of C17 and C19. *All Saints Church* has an Anglo-Saxon doorway which may contain remains of a church built there in the C8. Inside the church, in the recess of the doorway, there is a carving in stone of the heads of two dragons both biting a ball, probably dating back to the C11.

There is a footpath from the church which leads to Kemble Mill and to the river.

South Cerney (Map B1) off A419 4 m. S of Cirencester
P.O.|Shops|Pubs with food|Garage|Cotswold Water Park—lake for dinghies, fishing, swimming pools, tennis, caravanning, camping
The river Churn flows through the centre of the village which is large and well-kept with a wide main street (Silver St). Gravel has been extracted from extensive pits round the village and maps of the area now show huge square-shaped lakes which have replaced the fields and farms. Some of the lakes are used for water sports and other recreations but the extent of the lakes is so vast that it is difficult to imagine how use can be made of all of it. However, it is refreshing to see how quickly the barren shores of these man-made pools become covered by grass, rushes, trees and bushes, and birds are soon to be seen on the water.

The Churn is crossed by the road entering the village from the N and on either side of the bridge there are pubs serving food. By the side of the river at this point the quaintly named Bow-Wow Lane runs along the Churn and this makes a pleasant walk. Silver St has a number of houses of the C16/19 and Station Rd a row of C16/17 cottages with gables and mullions.
All Hallows Church is in a cul-de-sac with the Manor House, the Old Vicarage and Atkyns Manor (C17/18) nearby. The church has Norman, transitional and decorated features and was restored

in 1862 when the spire, badly damaged by lightning in 1857, was removed. The greatest treasure in the church is a C12 wooden carved head and foot, once part of a three-ft figure on a crucifix, now housed in a glass case on the N wall. This was discovered in 1915 buried in the NE wall of the Nave having been concealed at the time of the Reformation. Unfortunately the hiding place was damp and the rest of the crucifix had decayed. It is possible that it was made in Spain and brought home by a pilgrim to the shrine of St James at Santiago de Compostela. An authority on wood carving describes it as 'a work of great intensity . . . the earliest piece of wood carving in the country'.

Southrop (Photo 46, Map B3) off A361
4 m. N of Lechlade
Pub with food
Southrop is a classic example of a village built of oolitic limestone mellowed into a colour which alters with the changing light, but always blending with the landscape.

The River Leach is on the edge of the village near the Manor House, built in the C16/17. There is a pleasant walk from the village to Eastleach. When visited, the *Swan*, by the green, provided excellent meals, at lunchtime and in the evenings.

St Peter's Church (1100), is a plain building with later additions. The Keble family lived locally for many centuries and John Keble was curate of the church from 1823 to 1825. He discovered the Norman font built into the S doorway and this is now considered to be one of the finest in the Cotswolds. It shows the Virtues trampling on the Vices and stabbing them with sword or spear, also a representation of Moses with the tablets of the Commandments. The carvings are said to show a French influence in

46 *Southrop—Dry-Stone Wall. There are few modern buildings in this charming village which has retained many fine cottages of C16/17 and large houses of the same periods which have been carefully maintained. The village has some very high dry-stone walls in exceptionally fine condition. This probably results from the presence in the village of a craftsman who is renowned for his skill in building these walls.*

the greater freedom of expression than is usual in similar fonts.

Stanton Harcourt (Map A4) on B4449 6 m. SE of Witney

P.O.│Shop│Pub with food│West Oxon Sailing Club

The Saxon village which stood here was called 'Stan-tun' (settlement near the stones). The Devil's Quoits, a late Neolithic monument in a settlement SE of the present village has now been destroyed by gravel extraction.

The Harcourt family added their name to the village when they acquired the lordship of Stanton in the middle of the C12. The original house was built between 1380 and 1470. Today only the Great Kitchen, Pope's Tower and the Gatehouse remain, the main house being deserted in 1688. In 1755 most of the stone was taken to Nuneham Courtenay by the 1st Viscount to build his new house in the new 'Palladian' style.

The remains have now been restored and the gardens recreated to enhance the old walls and medieval buildings. Formal gardens within the area of the original buildings, informal wild gardens round the old fish ponds, and arcades lined with nut trees give charming views to the distant hills.

The *Great Kitchen* (C14) is the most complete medieval domestic kitchen surviving in England. In *Pope's Tower* the poet completed the translation of the 5th book of Homer's Iliad in 1718 although at this time the house had been abandoned. The Gatehouse (1540), now part of the present house, was remodelled in 1868 and enlarged in 1953 when the Harcourts returned.

The gardens, Great Kitchen and part

47 *Steventon—The Causeway. This is a raised path paved with stones and lined with trees which runs for over a mile from E to W through the entire village. It was probably built in the C14 by monks from the Abbey of Bec in Normandy who at that time owned the village. A paved narrow walk continues from the end of Milton Lane and this leads eventually to Milton village by crossing a bridge over the A34, the roar of traffic contrasting oddly with the gentle country-side.*

65

Perhaps because of the somewhat grim picture which much of the town presents, eight street murals enliven the dull walls on which they have been painted. In keeping with the discouraging attitude of officialdom on street murals the Information Centre and Town Guide show nothing of these striking examples of folk art and it is difficult to obtain full information about them. This mural enlivens a particularly drab car park. It was painted in 1976 with financial assistance from a local brewery. During the painting, retired railwaymen from the nearby Railway Village regularly advised on the details of the locomotive.

of the house are open to the public at various times in the summer.

Church of St Michael stands in the grounds of the Manor, built about 1130, extensively altered in the C13, has several monuments to the Harcourt family in the s transept and many fine brasses.

Steventon (Photo 47, Map C5) on B4017 4 m. s of Abingdon
P.O. | Shops | Pubs with food | Restaurants | Fruit Farms on A4130 | *Garage*
Travellers passing through Steventon on the B4017 will see little of this unusually interesting village except the village green, bordered by magnificent trees. The green, still one of the largest in the country, was originally about twice the size and included the present allotments. The most outstanding feature in the village is *The Causeway* (Photo 47).

Sheep farming in the Middle Ages was so successful that the rich wool merchants and farmers built many fine houses on the road which runs parallel to the Causeway. *The Priory* (C16) founded by Henry I as a branch of the Abbey of Bec contains a hammer-beamed hall. Now a National Trust property, it is open to free viewing on Wed. from 2–6 p.m.

St Michael and All Angels Church part of which dates from the C14 has an ancient yew in the churchyard.

Mill Street leads to Mill Bridge by the Mill House which was a fulling mill and today stands in a charming spot—well worth a visit.

On the B4017 is the old Station Yard with station houses designed by Brunel. The station is now disused but at one time board meetings of the GWR were held here as Steventon was halfway between London and Bristol and there was not a station at Oxford.

Sutton Courtenay (Map B5) on B4016 3 m. s of Abingdon
P.O. | Shops | Pubs with food | Garage
All Saints Church Parish church, largely Norman with additions made in C14/15. Lord Asquith (Prime Minister 1908–1916) who lived in the houses now called *The Wharf* and *Walton House* is buried

in the adjoining churchyard. George Orwell is also buried there (as Eric Blair, his real name) at the end of an avenue of yews planted in his memory.

Didcot Power Station occupies 29% of the parish, agriculture 40%, sand and gravel extraction 12%.

The village was originally known as Sutton (meaning South Town) and became Sutton Courtenay when the family of the name came in 1191 during the reign of Richard I. The Doomsday Book lists 150 inhabitants. There was a great increase in the population in 1959–1961 when a large council estate was built between Milton and Harwell roads. In 1974 there were about 2,640 people in the parish.

The village is unusually rich in interesting houses which line the main streets of the old part of the village. A very charming backwater of the Thames is reached by a path behind Wharf House passing by *Sutton Pools*, fed by a number of weirs, and eventually leading to the main river and Culham lock and village.

Sutton Bridge, over the Thames, leading to the main Abingdon road, was built in 1807 and was a toll bridge in private hands until 1939. The green in the centre of the village, adjoining the church, has many fine chestnut trees which, in the spring and autumn, are particularly beautiful.

Swindon (Photo 48, Map C2) off M4 between junctions 15 and 16, at junction of A361, A419, A420
Tourist Infm.—32 The Arcade, David Murray John Building, Brunel Centre | *Parking*—numerous on perimeter of Brunel Centre | *Shopping*—all the facilities of a large town and the vast Brunel shopping centre. Main shopping area is pedestrianised. High arcades and covered walkways recall the engineering and railway past of the town. Plaza with a large enclosed space and a glazed, vaulted roof provides accommodation for exhibitions, art markets and street theatre. Streets in Swindon's old town, at the top of Victoria Hill, still contain individual shops and long established family businesses | *Bookshops*—Paper Back Parade, 5 Theatre Square; Rainbow

Bookshop, Edgeware Rd; W.H. Smith, Regent St; Swindon Bookshop, 186 Victoria Rd; Victoria Bookshops, 30 Wood St; Websters, 27 Regent St | *Town Museum*—Apsley House, Bath Rd | *Wyvern Theatre and Arts Centre* | *Railway Village and Railway Museum* off Faringdon Rd. Open to public, weekdays 10–1, 2–5, Sun. 2–5. One of the most comprehensive displays in the country of locomotives, pictures and other interesting objects connected with railways is to be seen in the Railway Museum. The original railway village consisted of 300 cottages designed by Matthew Digby Wyatt, the architect of Paddington Station. They were greatly superior to similar houses then being built in the N, having shapely chimneys and gables. The cottages were modernised between 1969 and 1980 leaving their character and appearance unchanged. Bathrooms, new kitchens and space heating were installed and various other improvements were made. The whole environment was also improved by resurfacing roads, improving street lighting and providing garages and parking spaces.

A *'Living Museum'*, 34 Faringdon Rd, next door to the Railway Museum, has not been modernised but has been decorated and furnished as it would have been in late Victorian times. The cottage is full of genuine Victorian articles with all the usual kitchen equipment, parlour and bedroom furniture.

Oasis Leisure Centre, North Star Avenue, caters for the whole family. Free-shaped swimming pool, under the biggest glazed dome in Britain, which provides paddling, diving and waves rolling through the pool from a wave-making machine. Cafeteria and bar adjoin the pool. Complex of sports halls contain six-rink indoor bowls, squash courts, rifle and archery range, cricket nets, keep-fit room. In the grounds are all-weather playing pitches and cycle speedway track.

Historical notes—People have lived on old Swindon Hill at least as far back as Neolithic times. Remains of Bronze Age and Iron Age people have been found in the area. The Romans settled here from C1 until C5 and they appear to have lived in Swindon itself. Pagan Anglo-Saxon remains have also been found in Old Swindon, showing that sheep-rearing was important in the area. Swindon was called by the first English settlers 'the hill on which swine were kept'.

William the Conqueror gave the Old Town in 1066 to Odo, Bishop of Bayeux—a prominent figure in the Bayeux Tapestry—and this is recorded in the Doomsday Book. In 1289 the town had become an important market centre and became known as Chipping Swindon. In succeeding centuries the town remained prosperous as a centre for the surrounding agricultural community. Its prosperity was also aided by quarries during the C17 which supplied stone to London and to other cities.

Communication has always been good in the area since the Romans built Ermin Way passing through the district from Silchester in Hampshire to Cirencester

49 *Thames and Severn Canal—Sapperton Tunnel Entrance, near Coates, below* Tunnel House Inn. *A plaque above the arch records that the portal was rebuilt in 1976/77 by the Stroud Water Thames and Severn Canal Trust and the entrance now has a handsome appearance. To reach this entrance of the canal turn right off the A433* sw *of Cirencester towards Coates, then left after about one and a half miles, passing under a railway bridge. Soon after there is a narrow road on the right leading to the* Tunnel House Inn. *The entrance to the tunnel is just below. The Tunnel House built in the late C18 housed the men digging the tunnel and then the bargemen, later becoming an inn.*

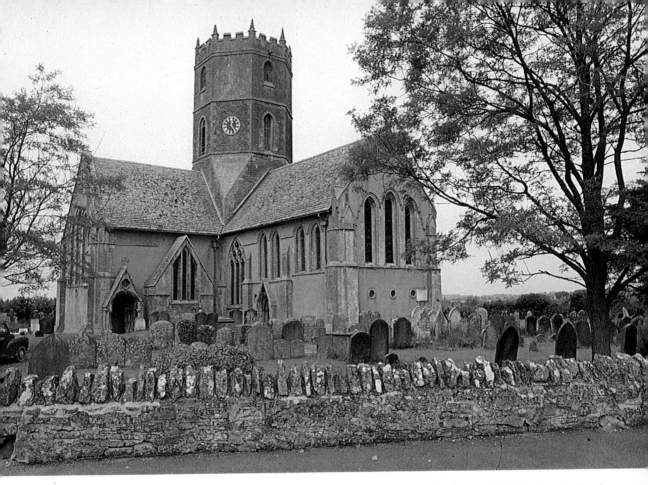

in Gloucestershire. The Coate reservoir, built in 1822 to supply water to the canal, is today used for sailing and fishing. Although Swindon is famous as a railway town it was not until 1835 that the GWR came, opened up a new life and created a new town. By 1842 the locomotive works were in production and Swindon became a railway centre.

Before 1894 Old and New Swindon were separate authorities with their own cemeteries, sewage works and fire engines. In 1900 the two Swindons were formed into one borough and in 1974 the Thamesdown Authority took over. Swindon is now the industrial and commercial centre of the Authority which has a population of about 150,000 and is still growing.

Murals in Swindon At present there are eight street murals in the town as listed below (owing to their transient nature the length of time that they will remain cannot be guaranteed):—1) St George and the Dragon, Manton St, 2) King Class Locomotive passing through Swindon Railway works, Henry St Car Park (Photo 48), 3) Golden Lion Bridge, Fleming Way, 4) Castle Combe, Cricklade Rd, 5) Bavarian Castle, 6) Children's Story Wall, Lethbridge Rd School, 7) Swindon Junction Railway Station 1901, 8) Swindon Celebrities, 1979, Union St.

Thames, source of (Photo back cover, Map B1)
The source of the Thames was at one time in dispute between Seven Springs (os ref. 969171, where the A435 and A436 cross) and Thames Head (os ref. 981995). Seven Springs is the source of the Churn which joins the Thames near Cricklade, and Thames Head in Trewsbury Mead is now considered to be the true source of the Thames. There is a lay-by before the railway bridge on the A433, 3 m. sw of Cirencester in which you should park. Walk back along the road for about 100 yds, cross the road and go through a five-barred

50 Uffington. St Mary's Church is an impressive building, known as 'Cathedral of the Vale'. The spire was destroyed by lightning in 1743 and was replaced by a further storey of the tower which is octagonal. The building is cruciform and is mostly mid-C13, probably designed by the same architect-mason who built Salisbury Cathedral since many details in the buildings are similar.

51 *Uffington. A chalk-built cottage with its thatched roof typical of the many charming buildings of this type in Uffington.*

gate. Carry on walking through a wide field, following a line of trees, and make for the edge of a small wood. There you will find a plaque erected by the Thames Conservancy to mark the source. In front of the plaque there is a ring of stones surrounding a depression which is usually dry but is the actual source. The water table is not far below the surface and adjoining meadows are often flooded. The statue of *Father Thames* (Photo back cover) which once stood here was removed to St John's Lock at Lechlade because of vandalism.

The Thames Head pub, serving meals, is on the A433 on the other side of the railway bridge from the lay-by.

Thames and Severn Canal (Photos 37, 49, Map B1)
Completed in 1789 after six years' work, it ran from Wallbridge near Stroud to Inglesham on the Thames, cost about

£250,000, had forty-four locks and the 3rd longest canal tunnel (over two m.) running through the Cotswolds, and carried barges up to seventy ft long and seven ft wide along its total length of nearly twenty-nine m.

The Canal closed in 1893 having been bought by the GWR, probably to stop competition. A restoration in 1895 was a failure and although the Gloucestershire County Council spent more money on it there was little traffic. The last barge travelled through in 1911 and the entire canal ceased operation in 1933. In some areas there is now little trace of the bed of the canal although the round houses built for canal men still stand.

Uffington (Photos 50, 51, Map C4) off B4507 7 m. **w** of Wantage
P.O. | Shop | Pubs with food | Garage
This is a chalk and thatch village overlooked by the White Horse, with an

interesting history, where four roads meet. In 1285 Edward I stopped the villagers from holding fairs and markets in the churchyard 'for the sake of the church'. At Uffington Feast wrestling and backswording took place on raised wooden platforms. Backswording was fought with wooden cudgels and broken heads and bruises were very common. Thomas Hughes, author of 'Tom Brown's Schooldays' and 'Scouring of the White Horse', born in Uffington in 1822, lived with his grandfather, vicar of the church, and gives detailed descriptions of the dress and occupations of the people in the village in his books.

Uffington School (early C17), built of chalk, with mullioned windows, is now used as a reading room and referred to as 'Tom Brown's School'.

Wallingford (Photo 52, Map C6) at junction of A329 and A4130
Market Day—Fri. | *Tourist Infm.*—Stone House, High St | *Parking*—ample | *Toilets*—High St, Market Place, Wood St | *P.O.* | *Banks* | *Garages* | *Shopping*—good variety including supermarkets; Lamb Arcade, High St, is an unusually attractive shopping centre with antique, craft and book shops also a coffee shop serving excellent light meals in pleasant and quiet surroundings, and a wine vault serving meals. Headquarters of Habitat is in St John's Rd on the sw outskirts of town | *Bookshops*—Colophon, St Mary's St; Bookshop, 10c St Martins St | *Pubs* | *Hotels* | *Restaurants* | *Cafés*—a good variety | *Museum*—Flint House, High St, Open Tues.–Fri., Sun. 2–5 p.m., Sat. 10.30–12.30, 2–5 | *Cinema*—Corn Exchange, Market Place | *Theatre*—Corn Exchange; Kinecroft Theatre | *Sporting Facilities*—Swimming, open air pool by river; Riverside caravan and camping site, near river | *Boats for hire* at Wallingford Bridge Boat House and Maidboats.

Wallingford's history began in Roman

52 *Wallingford—Bridge and spire of St Peter's Church. The bridge dates from the Saxon period and contains material from various centuries. It brought trade to the town as the most reliable crossing over the Thames, providing a safe route between London and the w. When Abingdon built its bridge in 1422 this provided a nearer crossing and thereafter the prosperity of Wallingford declined.*

times and it was an important town in the C9, fortified by King Alfred. Remains of the Saxon earthworks can still be seen enclosing a recreation ground on the w side of the town off the High St. The regular pattern of the streets which still exists was probably first laid out by Alfred. For over three hundred years there was a Royal Mint in the town and coins were minted there until 1270.

After the Norman conquest Robert D'Oyley built a castle later demolished by Cromwell. The remains of the castle are now in private hands and not open to the public. In 1285 there were fourteen churches (only three remain), and a priory (demolished in 1525). After this time there were disastrous plagues, including the Black Death of 1349. The decline in trade was hastened when Abingdon bridge was built in 1422. Until then the town had many thriving inns as the main road from London to Wales and Gloucester went across Wallingford Bridge. The bridge, built at various times, 300 yds long, has sixteen arches including nine in the Oxford approach, not counting three small culverts.

During the Civil War the castle was held for Charles I and when captured by Cromwell he ordered it to be completely destroyed. The town continued to decline and it was not until the C18 that any further significant building took place. Trade in the town also increased and malting became a major industry. As farming in the area became prosperous the market revived. Today Wallingford is a pleasant small town with good shops and many attractive buildings. As in other towns near the Atomic Energy Research Establishment at Harwell it has benefited from the influx of the scientists and their families into the area.

Town Hall built in 1670, stands in the Market Place, has an open ground floor with four columns.

53 *Wantage—Market Place and King Alfred's Statue. The Market Place, in which a market is held on Wed. and Sat., has a wide variety of buildings, nearly all occupied by shops, around its wide irregular shape. Brick, stucco and timber facings provide a variety of styles to give an interesting look to the whole area. The name*

St Mary's Church stands s of the Market Place. Built of flint mostly in 1854, the w tower with polygonal angle buttresses built in 1653 probably from remains of the castle, demolished by Cromwell.

St Leonard's Church Oldest church in the town, damaged by Cromwell's soldiers and by fire during the Civil War, restored 1849.

St Peter's Church built 1769 in classical style, similar to Wren's city church of St Bride's Fleet St—the elegant spire added in 1777 gives the church, in its riverside setting, a most unusual and pleasing appearance.

Wantage (Photo 53, Map C4) at junction of A338 and A417

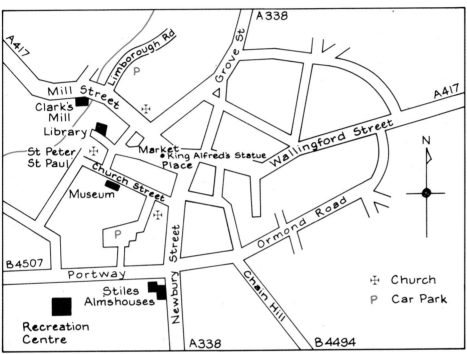

Wantage is probably derived from the Old English word 'wanian' (to decrease) and meaning 'intermittent stream'. There was a Roman settlement here but not one of great importance although the Romans paved part of the Icknield Way (now Portway) which leads from the town. In early Saxon times there was a settlement and the Kings of Wessex had a palace here, of which nothing now remains. Alfred the Great was born at Wantage in 849 and his imposing statue now stands in the Market Place. Colonel Loyd-Lindsay, VC, of Lockinge (later Lord Wantage) raised the money for the statue, providing most of the cost himself. It was designed by Count Gleichen and erected in 1877.

Market Days—Wed. and Sat. | *Tourist Infm.*—Vale and Downland Museum, Church St | *Parking*—Limborough Rd and Portway | *Toilets* | *Shopping*—wide range of usual shops and supermarkets | *Bookshop*—Miller's, Mill St | *P.O.* | *Banks* | *Garage* | *Garden Centre* | *Pubs* | *Hotels* | *Restaurants* | *Cafés*—a good variety | *Recreation Centre*—Portway (swimming pool, sauna, various indoor sports) | *Museum*—Vale and Downland Museum in Church St (opposite church) was opened in September 1983. It was converted from a C17 cloth-merchant's house and extended by a new building with wooden crucks spanning two floors. A reconstructed Downland barn houses a collection of agricultural machinery and equipment. In the main building there is a fine display covering the history, the buildings and the industries of the Vale and Downland.

Church of St Peter and St Paul which replaced a Saxon and Norman church which stood on the same site, dates mostly from late C13. Restoration carried out in 1857 by George Edmund Street, a local architect. Has a C15 s porch, a hammerbeam roof with massive piers and arches supporting the central tower. Contains eleven fine Fitzwarren brasses and a magnificent alabaster tomb to Sir Ivo Fitzwarren and his wife.

An inscription on the base of the larger-than-life statue of King Alfred in the Market Place summarises his achievements: 'ALFRED THE GREAT/The West Saxon King, born at Wantage, AD

849/Alfred found learning dead,/
And he restored it./Education neg-
lected,/And he revived it,/The laws
powerless./And he gave them force./The
Church debased,/And he raised it./The
land ravaged by a fearful enemy/From
which he delivered it./Alfred's name
will live as long as mankind shall respect
the past.'

Until about 1840 when the railway
came through the Vale of the White
Horse, Wantage was a remote town and
was known as 'Black Wantage'. It was
said that thieves driven out from London
took refuge in the town which also had
an unruly element in the 'navigators'
(navvies) who dug the Wilts and Berks
canal. Local administration was in the
nominal hands of a lord of the manor
who did little to control the violence
and it was not until the inhabitants of
Wantage organised their own affairs
that matters improved.

The town contains a number of mellow
C18 houses built of blue and red bricks
from the Challow brickworks nearby.
The railway station was opened in 1840
but was about four miles from the town,
and a later station about two miles away
was built in 1863. A horse bus, replaced
in 1876 by a steam locomotive, took
people to the station, the first to run a
regular passenger service by mechanical
traction. The last locomotive to be used
on the track was a George England
Well Tank Locomotive called 'Jane'
(official name 'Shannon'). This faithful
and efficient tank engine pulled the
train from 1878 to 1945 when the line
was removed. 'Jane' is now preserved in
the Railway Museum at Didcot.

In 1860 there were three mills in
Wantage and *Clark's Mill* is still working
at the bottom of Mill St. It was originally
powered by Letcombe Brook which
flows through the building. A gas engine
is now installed and the mill grinds
about 180 tons of flour every week from
local soft wheat and Canadian hard
wheat. This flour is used by local bakers
and is also on sale in small quantities at
the mill.

Flax and hemp were grown in the
Vale of the White Horse in about 1800
and weaving and rope-making were
flourishing trades. The clear water of

Letcombe Brook was ideal for washing
the cloth. Tanning was also an important
industry at that time in Wantage and
the tan yard between Grove St and
Garston Lane was one of the largest and
most modern in England.

The *Ridgeway Path* is about two m. s
of the town on the A338 or B4494.

John Betjeman, the late Poet Laureate,
who lived near Wantage, has written
several poems about the area, including
'Wantage Bells', 'On Leaving Wantage
1972' and 'Uffington'.

Warborough (Map B6) on A329 2 m. E
of Dorchester
Shops | Pubs with food
Pretty village with half-timbered cottages
and a large green on which cricket is
played. Across the green there is a distant
view of the Chilterns. The thatched pub
on the edge of the green provides meals
and serves Brakspear's, a first-class
Henley beer.

St Laurence Church is W of the green
and contains a pulpit and the C17 and a
late-C12 lead font.

West Hendred (Map C5) off A417 3 m.
E of Wantage
P.O. | Shop | Pub with food
Stands at the foot of the Downs with
the Ginge Brook running through the
village. There is one main road which
leads up to a path to the Downs and
the Ridgeway. The houses are mostly
small with timber frames, brick and
cream-washed walls, making a pleasing
picture.

Beryl Maile, a painter and teacher
with wide ranging skills, has a studio in
the village where her work is for sale
and where she holds art courses and
demonstrations. She has a bold and
exciting approach to painting which
succeeds in capturing by vigorous com-
position the landscapes of the Downland
countryside.

Holy Trinity Church stands by the
brook in a field at the S edge of the
village. It was built in the decorated
style with additions in C15. The altar
rail, pulpit, reading desk and font cover
are Jacobean.

Witney (Photo 54, Map A4) at junction of A415 and A4095

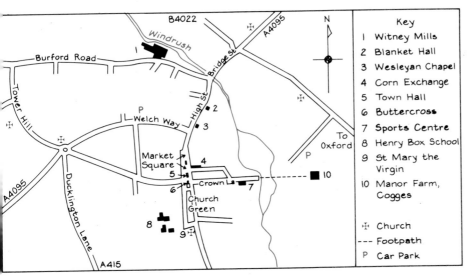

Key
1 Witney Mills
2 Blanket Hall
3 Wesleyan Chapel
4 Corn Exchange
5 Town Hall
6 Buttercross
7 Sports Centre
8 Henry Box School
9 St Mary the Virgin
10 Manor Farm, Cogges

✠ Church
--- Footpath
P Car Park

Market Days—Thurs. and Sat.|*Tourist Infm.*—Town Hall, Market Square| *Parking*—Welch Way, free|*Toilets*— Welch Way|*P.O.*|*Banks*|*Garages*| *Shopping*—Supermarket and good range of other shops|*Bookshop*—Witney Bookseller, High St, W.H. Smith, High St|*Hotels*|*Restaurants*|*Pubs*|*Cafés*| *Cinema*—Market Square|*Sports Centre*— Crown Lane (swimming, squash)

St Mary the Virgin Church The impressive Early English tower of the church with a spire of 156 ft stands at the s end of a large wedge-shaped medieval green formerly used as a market place. Entirely rebuilt during the early C13 on the site of a Saxon church with additions made during the C14/15. Drastic restoration was made in the 1860s which left the interior with its rather bare and chilling appearance. The N transept has a seven-light decorated window reaching the roof. This window is probably the finest in the country.

Witney has a strong Protestant tradition and supported Parliament during the Civil War. Methodism is still strong in Witney and there is a large Wesleyan Church in the High St seating 900 people.

Henry Box School a handsome C17 building with additions in 1970 stands by the side of Church Green. Founded in 1660 by Henry Box it is now a comprehensive school.

Blanket Hall, High St built in 1721 in baroque style—a relic of the Witney Blanket Weavers Company which was a craft guild formed in 1711. All the blankets made in Witney at that time were weighed and measured here. There is an interesting one-handed clock on the pediment and a wooden bell-turret with a cupola.

Manor Farm Museum, Cogges, can be reached by walking down Crown Lane, off the Market Place, or by car off B4022 (parking near Museum), open March to end of October daily 10–6.

Cogges is a 'Museum of Farming', but is not in any sense a collection of dead artefacts: it is run as a going concern where all the occupations of a typical Edwardian farm are carried on. Laundry work, bread- and butter-making can be seen in the farm buildings; and outside, the crafts of hurdle-making, steam-threshing, black-smithing and sheep-shearing are practised as well as many other activities. Waggons, horse-drawn implements and hand-tools on exhibition illustrate the farming methods in Edwardian days.

The Doomsday Book records a settlement here and later there was a priory, a medieval manor house, fishponds and

54 *Witney—Butter Cross and Town Hall, Market Place. The Butter Cross was 'erected in 1683 by Gulielmus Blake Armiger of Cogges' according to an inscription which appears on a medallion on the cupola but this is thought to relate only to the clock-turret. The main building was probably built at an earlier date and until the Reformation it was a religious shrine. It later provided a covered area for selling goods. The C17 Town Hall has an open-pillared ground floor in which corn factors bought and sold grain, with an assembly hall above.*

a mill. An historical trail which marks the remains of these buildings can be followed by visitors, and pleasant walks follow the River Windrush which flows by the farm.

The town developed because it was planned by successive Bishops of Winchester who also laid out the large triangular market area which now forms the Church Green. Witney prospered as a market town and by the end of the Middle Ages it was a centre for cloth- and blanket-making. The Black Death killed about two-thirds of the population but in 1677 there were sixty 'blanketers' and 150 looms employing about 3000 people. The water in the Windrush was used to cleanse and thicken the wool for the blankets and it was said to give the cloth a unique whiteness. Sadly the Witney blanket trade has today declined although fine blankets are still made in the town. Other industries, such as light engineering, have now been established in the town.

Wolvercote and **Port Meadow** (Photo 55, Map A5) off A34 and A40 3 m. N of centre of Oxford
P.O.|Shop|Pubs|Motels
Wolvercote is a straggling village: the upper part is a modern residential suburb of Oxford, and the lower part, on the side of the railway leading down to the river, is the original village (see **Godstow**).

The suburban half contains two modern motels, both adjoining the bypass. The Pear Tree Motor Lodge looks like a holiday camp and is an odd sight to encounter as one approaches Oxford. The Oxford Motel is on the way to Lower Wolvercote and is more restrained in design.

On a bridge over a backwater overlooking Port Meadow there is a plaque commemorating the two RFC men who died in a wrecked monoplane 100 yds N of this spot on September 10th 1912.

Port Meadow, between Wolvercote and Oxford is about 342 acres and has

provided pasture for the animals of the freemen of Oxford at least since the C11. The actual ownership of the land has been in dispute for centuries and only in 1970 was it registered as common land. The freemen may only pasture animals on the Meadow and are not allowed to take turf or gravel from it. By 1970 there were 210 registered freemen who shared grazing rights for pasturing about 700 beasts. This vast Meadow, which is bordered on one side by the Thames, floods in winter, has herons, large flocks of geese and provides fine views of the spires of Oxford.

Woolstone (Photo 56, Map C3) off B4507 7 m. **w** of Wantage
Pub with food
This village is full of delights for the eye and spirit as well as providing, by its many varieties of splendid trees,

welcome shade on a hot day.

The traditional cottages with their timber frames, chalk and brick walls, and thatched roofs all combine to give a mellow, restful feeling, set as they are in a hollow with a stream from the Manger running through the village.

St Peter's Church a Chapel of Ease for Uffington, has a nave and chancel which are surprisingly and happily lit by a window near the pulpit and four windows in the chancel, inserted in 1330 just before the Black Death. In 1954 the chalk blocks of the chancel walls were covered in plaster and then covered by a silver whitewash. The effect of these two improvements, with 600 yrs interval, is quite dramatic since the church is flooded with light. The main parts of the church were built in C13 of chalk blocks taken from a quarry on the Downs less than a mile away and local Sarsen stones were used on the lower

55 Wolvercote. The grave of J.R.R. Tolkien (author of 'The Lord of the Rings') who died in 1973 and his wife is in Wolvercote cemetery which is entered from the Oxford/Banbury Road (A423). Large numbers of members of Tolkien clubs visit the grave on the anniversary of his death. It is ironic that the creator of the fantasy world of 'The Lord of the Rings' should be buried in a mundane suburban cemetery with a prosaic marble headstone and surround.

part of the walls and as footings for the foundations.

A fine sculpture of the Stations of the Cross in the transept, designed, modelled and cast in metal-filled polyester resin reinforced with glass fibre by a villager, Mrs M.U. Lloyd, was installed in 1968. It is heartening to see, in this ancient building, a modern work of great force and impact, which revives the medieval tradition of showing in the church the events of the Christian story.

Wytham (Map A5) off A34 2 m. NW of Oxford
P.O.|Shop|Pub with food
Oxford University owns the village apart from the church, the rectory, the school and the *White Hart*, and no building is allowed which is not compatible with the rest of the village. Consequently, although it is very well preserved, there is an air of time having been frozen in the place. The stone cottages and walls are beautifully kept and the pub and its garden are in keeping with the rest of the village.

All Saints Church The entrance to the church has a stone square-headed doorway taken from Cumnor Place (where Amy Robsart died) and another leads to a church garden. The church was largely rebuilt in 1814 by Lord Abingdon using some more material from Cumnor Place. The Manor House adjoining the church has now been turned into flats and is not open to the public.

Wytham Woods partly bordering the Thames cover more than 600 acres and are also owned by Oxford University. The woods are maintained under a deed which ensures that 'every care should be taken to preserve the woods in their present state of natural beauty'. Access is limited to members of the University. The University Field Station lies N of the village.

56 Woolstone—White Horse Inn. After viewing White Horse Hill the visitor goes down Woolstone Hill and into Woolstone village, where refreshment is available at the White Horse Inn, a romantic, handsome building timber-framed, brick-filled and tiled.

TOURIST INFORMATION

Arts & Crafts—Ardington, Bampton, Cirencester, Filkins, West Hendred
Houses, Gardens, National Trust Properties open to the public—Buscot, Coleshill, Cotswold Wildlife Park, Great Coxwell, Kelmscott, Kingston Bagpuize, Kingston Lisle, Milton, Nuneham Courtenay, Pusey, Stanton Harcourt, Steventon, Wayland's Smithy, White Horse Hill

Museums—Abingdon, Cirencester, Cricklade, Didcot, Dorchester on Thames, East Hendred, Kemble, Long Wittenham, Swindon, Wallingford, Wantage, Witney
Sporting Activities—Abingdon, Cirencester, Cricklade, Cumnor, Dorchester on Thames, Fairford, Lechlade, Radcot Bridge, Somerford Keynes, South Cerney, Stanton Harcourt, Swindon, Wallingford, Wantage, Witney

SELECT BIBLIOGRAPHY

ANDERSON, J R L *The Upper Thames* (Eyre Methuen) 1974

ANDERSON, J R L and GODWIN, FAY *The Oldest Road: An Exploration of the Ridgeway* (Wildwood House) 1975

BATEY, MAVIS *Oxford Gardens* (Avebury) 1982

BECKINSDALE, ROBERT and MONICA *The English Heartland* (Duckworth) 1980

BETJEMAN, JOHN and PIPER, JOHN *Murray's Berkshire—Architectural Guide* (John Murray) 1949

BLOXHAM, CHRISTINE *Portrait of Oxfordshire* (R. Hale) 1982

BRUNSKILL, R W *Illustrated Handbook of Vernacular Architecture* (Faber and Faber) 1978

CHERRY, B and BONNEY, D *The Buildings of England—Wiltshire* (Penguin Books) 1976

CLIFTON-TAYLOR, ALEC and IRESON, A S *English Stone Building* (Gollancz) 1983

EAGLE, DOROTHY and CARNELL, HILARY *The Oxford Literary Guide to the British Isles* (OUP) 1977

EMERY, FRANK *The Oxfordshire Landscape* (Hodder and Stoughton) 1974

HAMMOND, NIGEL *The White Horse Country* (Countryside Books) 1972

HAMMOND, NIGEL *Rural Life in the Vale of the White House 1780–1914* (Countryside Books) 1974

HARVEY, NIGEL *The Industrial Archaeology of Farming in England and Wales* (Batsford) 1980

HOSKINS, W G *The Making of the English Landscape* (Penguin Books) 1970

JESSUP, MARY *A History of Oxfordshire* (Phillimore) 1975

JONES, MARTIN and DIMBLEBY, GEOFFREY (Editors) *The Environment of Man: the Iron Age to the Anglo-Saxon Period* (BAR British Series 87) 1981

METCALFE, LEON *Discovering the Thames* (Shire Pubns) 1981

MORRIS, JAN *Oxford* (OUP) 1978

PEEL, J H B *Portrait of the Thames* (R. Hale) 1967

PEVSNER, NIKOLAUS *The Buildings of England—Berkshire* (Penguin Books) 1966

PHILLIPS, GEOFFREY *Thames Crossings, Bridges, Tunnels and Ferries* (David and Charles) 1981

PRICHARD, MARI and CARPENTER, HUMPHREY *A Thames Companion* (OUP) 1981

ROWLEY, TREVOR *Villages in the Landscape* (Dent) 1978

ROWLEY, TREVOR (Editor) *The Oxford Region* (O.U. Department for External Studies) 1981

SEEBOHM, M E *The Evolution of the English Farm* (E.P. Publishing) 1976

SHARP, DAVID *The Thames Walk* (Ramblers' Association) 1981

SHERWOOD, JENNIFER and PEVSNER, NIKOLAUS *The Buildings of England—Oxfordshire* (Penguin Books) 1974

THACKER, FRED S *The Thames Highway*: volume one—*General History*: volume two—*Locks and Weirs* (David and Charles) 1968

TOWNSEND, JAMES *A History of Abingdon* (Henry Frowde) 1910

VEREY, D *The Buildings of England—Gloucestershire*: volume one *Cotswolds* (Penguin Books) 1970

VICTORIA HISTORY OF THE COUNTIES OF ENGLAND: *History of the County of Oxford*: volume four *The City of Oxford* (OUP) 1979

UPPER THAMES VALLEY TODAY

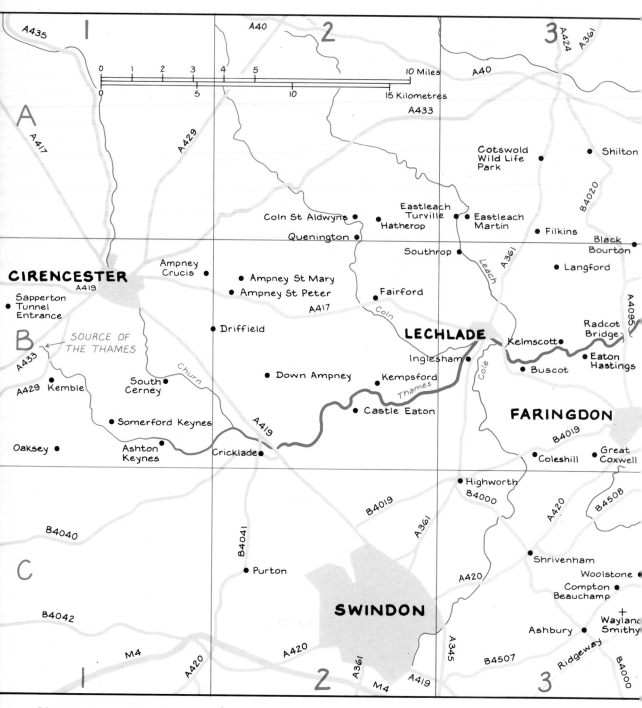

PLACE-NAME INDEX